STAR WARS

THE FORCE UNLEASHED II

The Rise of the Empire (1,000 - 0 years before the battle of Yavin)
After the seeming final defeat of the Sith, the Republic enters a state of complacency. In the waning years of the Republic, the Senate rife with corruption, the ambitious Senator Palpatine causes himself to be elected Supreme Chancellor. This is the era of the prequel trilogy.

The events in this story take place approximately twelve months before the Battle of Yavin.

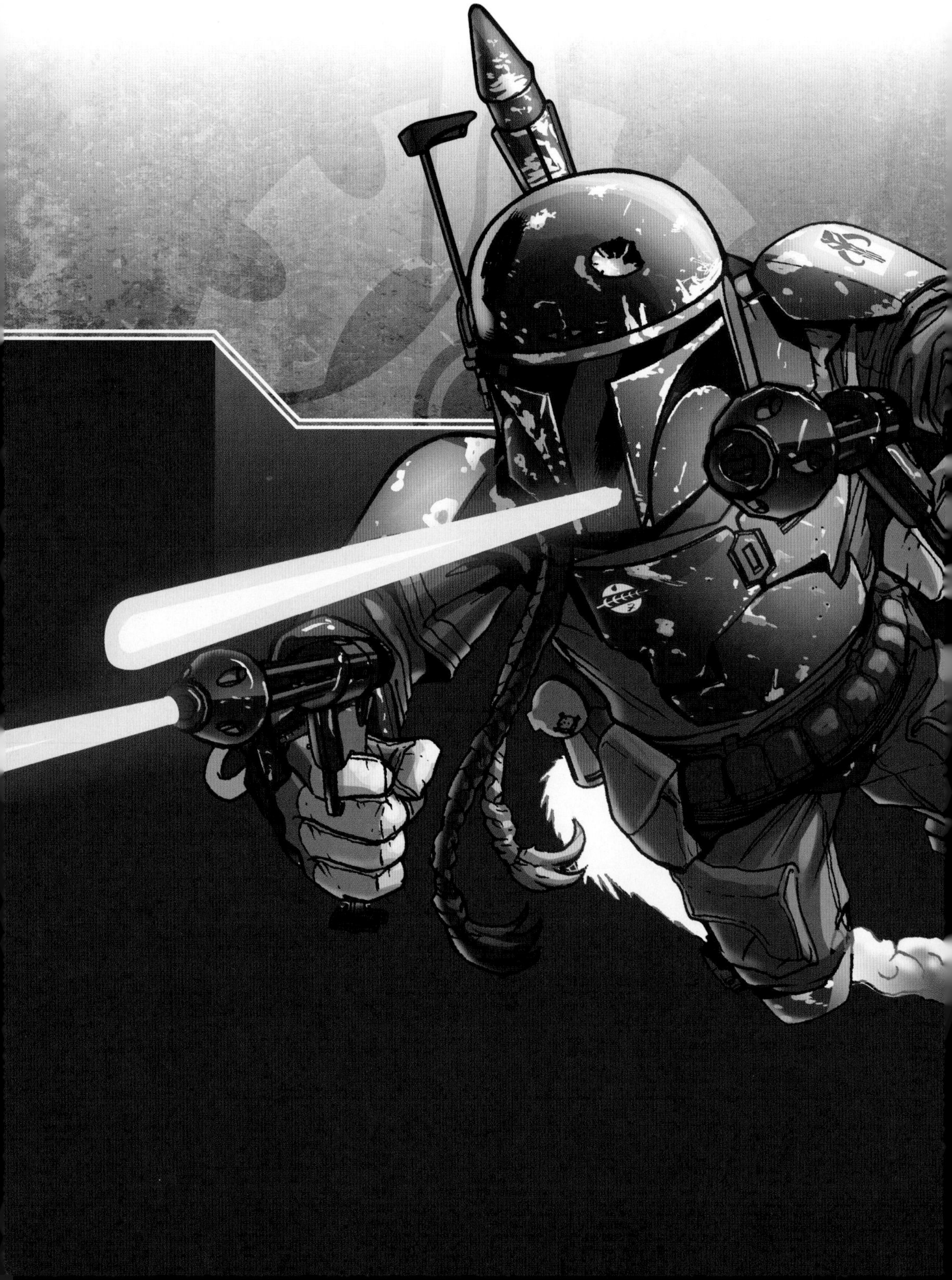

STAR WARS® THE FORCE UNLEASHED™ II

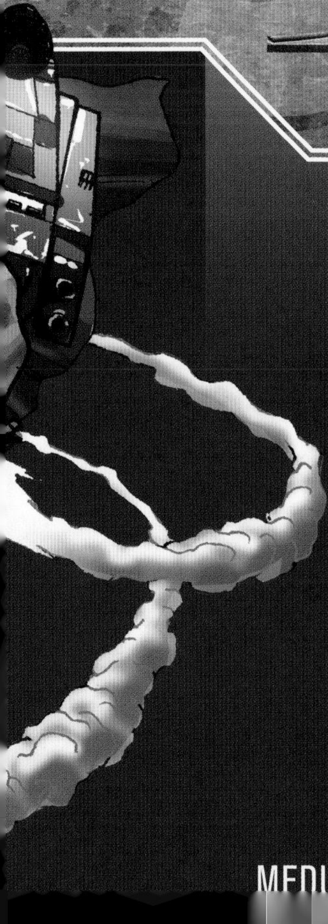

script
HADEN BLACKMAN

art
OMAR FRANCIA
with MANUEL SILVA

colors
DIEGO RODRIGUEZ

letters
MICHAEL HEISLER

cover
MEDUZARTS DIGITAL ENVIRONMENT STUDIO

president and publisher
MIKE RICHARDSON

collection designers
STEPHEN REICHERT and SCOTT COOK

editor
RANDY STRADLEY

assistant editor
FREDDYE LINS

special thanks to Jann Moorhead, David Anderman, Troy Alders,
Leland Chee, Sue Rostoni, and Carol Roeder at Lucas Licensing

NEIL HANKERSON executive vice president TOM WEDDLE chief financial officer RANDY STRADLEY
vice president of publishing MICHAEL MARTENS vice president of business development ANITA NELSON
vice president of business affairs MICHA HERSHMAN vice president of marketing DAVID SCROGGY vice
president of product development DALE LAFOUNTAIN vice president of information technology DARLENE
VOGEL director of purchasing KEN LIZZI general counsel DAVEY ESTRADA editorial director SCOTT
ALLIE senior managing editor CHRIS WARNER senior books editor DIANA SCHUTZ executive editor CARY
GRAZZINI director of design and production LIA RIBACCHI art director CARA NIECE director of scheduling

STAR WARS: THE FORCE UNLEASHED II

Published by
Dark Horse Books
A division of Dark Horse Comics, Inc.
10956 SE Main Street
Milwaukie, OR 97222

darkhorse.com
starwars.com

To find a comics shop in your area,
call the Comic Shop Locator Service toll-free at 1-888-266-4226

First edition: October 2010
ISBN: 978-1-59582-553-7

1 3 5 7 9 10 8 6 4 2

Printed at Midas Printing International, Ltd., Huizhou, China

INTRODUCTION

A year ago, enemies of the Empire officially formed the Rebel
Alliance to restore the galaxy to the Republic.

First brought together by a Force-wielding stranger, Starkiller—who
was once the secret apprentice of Darth Vader—the leadership of
the Rebellion barely survived a battle with Vader and the Emperor
which led to Starkiller's death.

Now, Darth Vader is preoccupied with thoughts of his apprentice
and one of Starkiller's deranged clones, who poses a threat to the
Empire's plans. To aid him in his search for the rogue clone, Vader
hires the galaxy's greatest bounty hunter: Boba Fett!

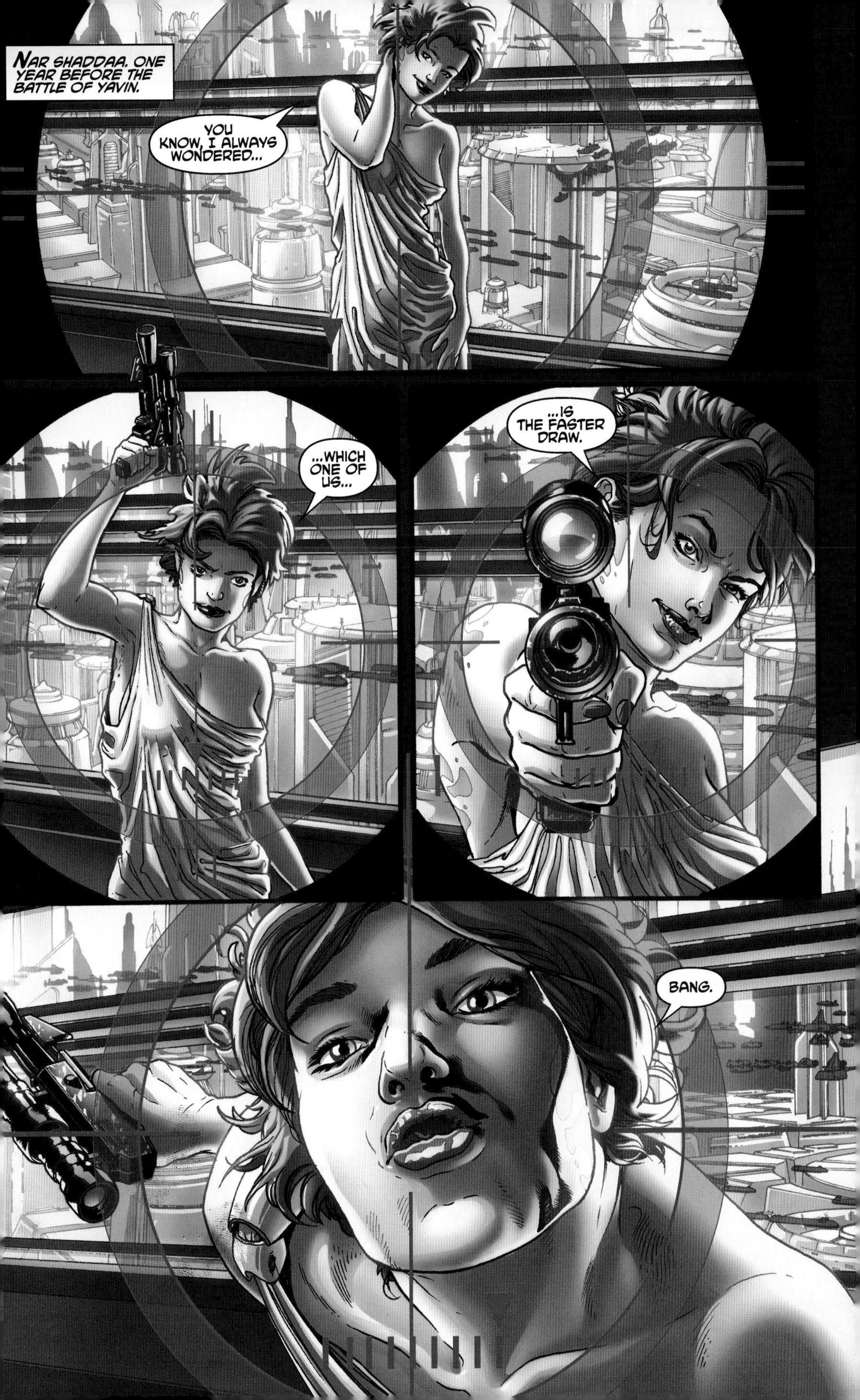
NAR SHADDAA. ONE YEAR BEFORE THE BATTLE OF YAVIN.
YOU KNOW, I ALWAYS WONDERED...
...WHICH ONE OF US...
...IS THE FASTER DRAW.
BANG.

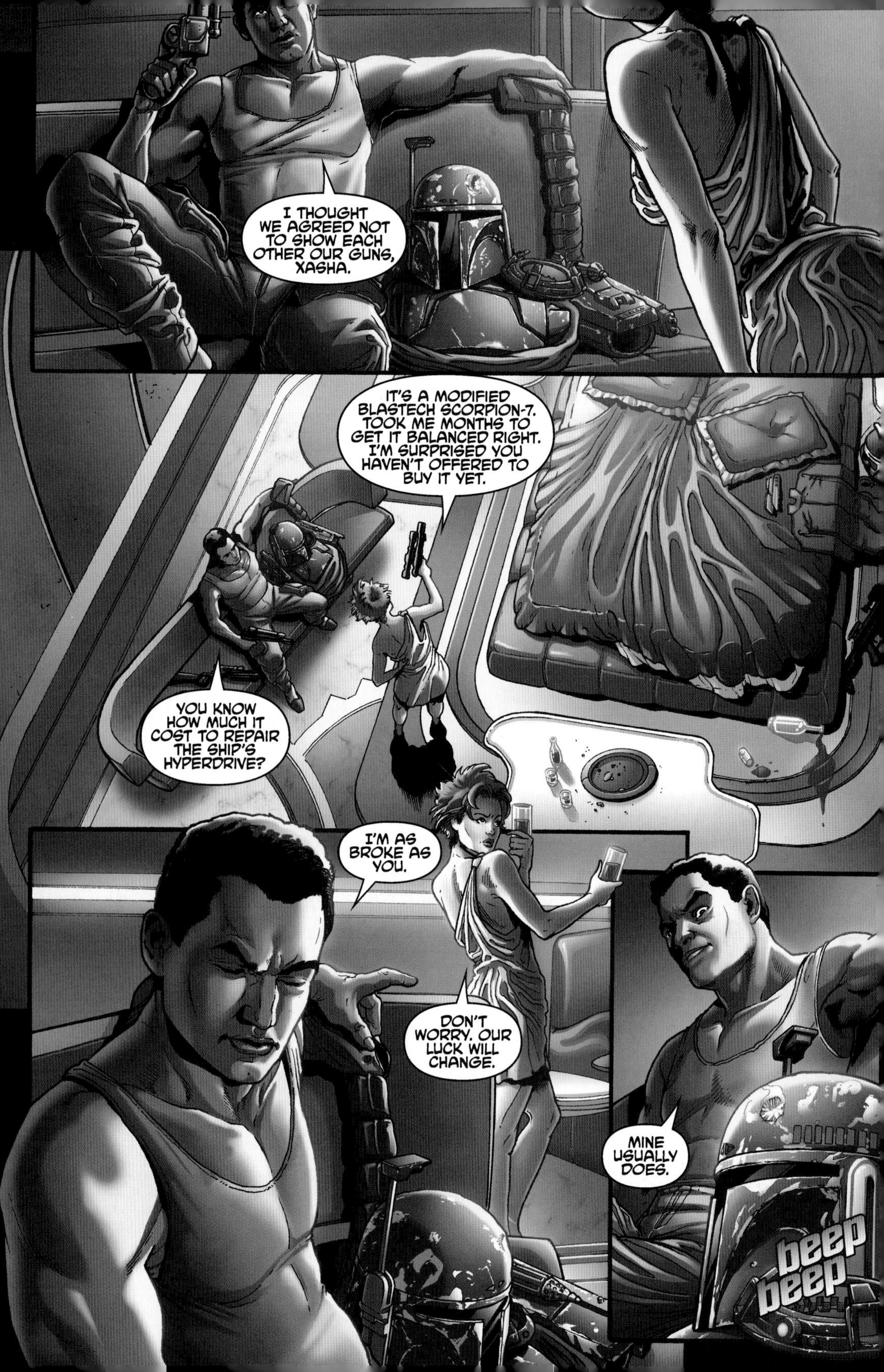
I THOUGHT WE AGREED NOT TO SHOW EACH OTHER OUR GUNS, XASHA.
IT'S A MODIFIED BLASTECH SCORPION-7. TOOK ME MONTHS TO GET IT BALANCED RIGHT. I'M SURPRISED YOU HAVEN'T OFFERED TO BUY IT YET.
YOU KNOW HOW MUCH IT COST TO REPAIR THE SHIP'S HYPERDRIVE?
I'M AS BROKE AS YOU.
DON'T WORRY. OUR LUCK WILL CHANGE.
MINE USUALLY DOES.
beep beep

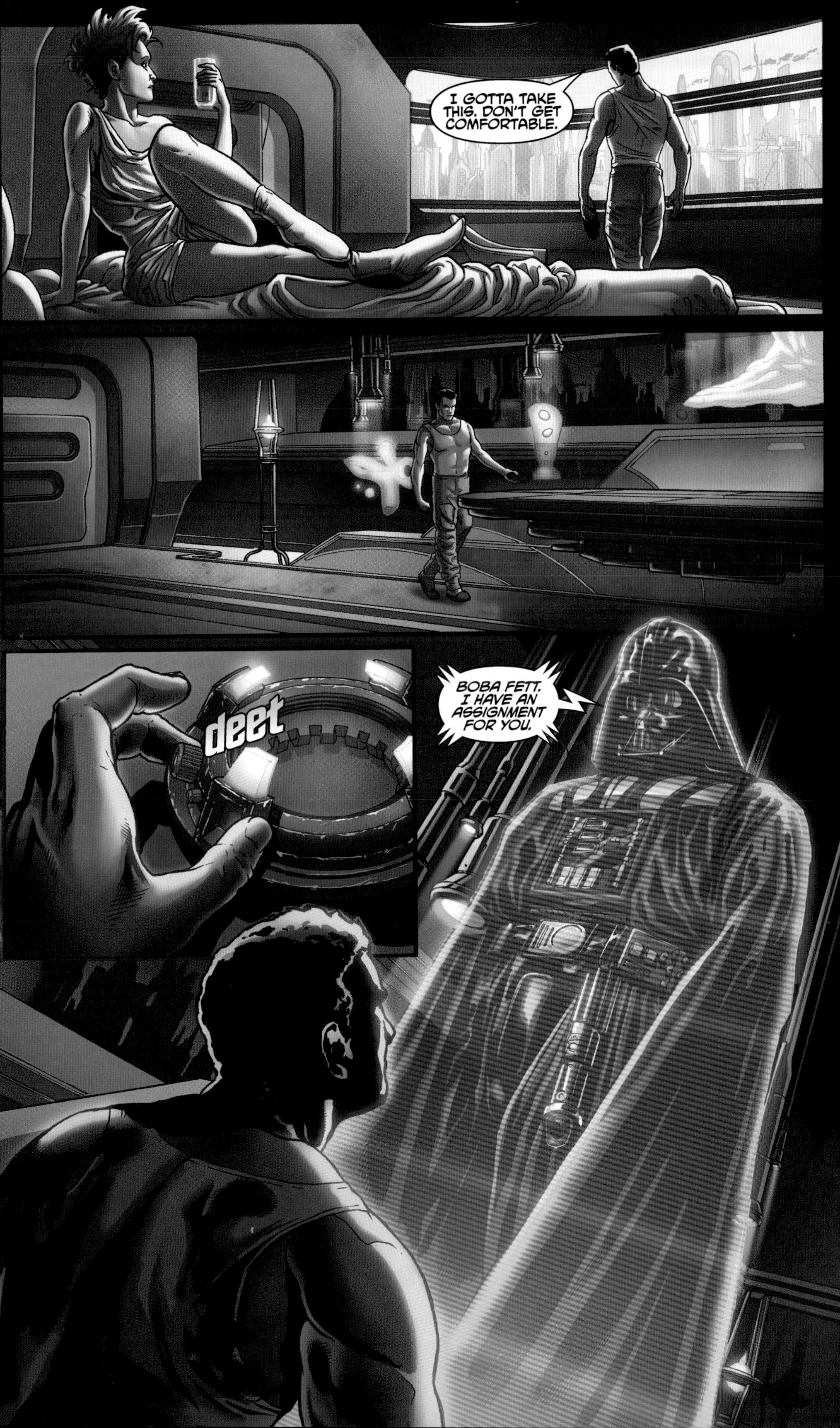
I GOTTA TAKE THIS. DON'T GET COMFORTABLE.
deet
BOBA FETT. I HAVE AN ASSIGNMENT FOR YOU.

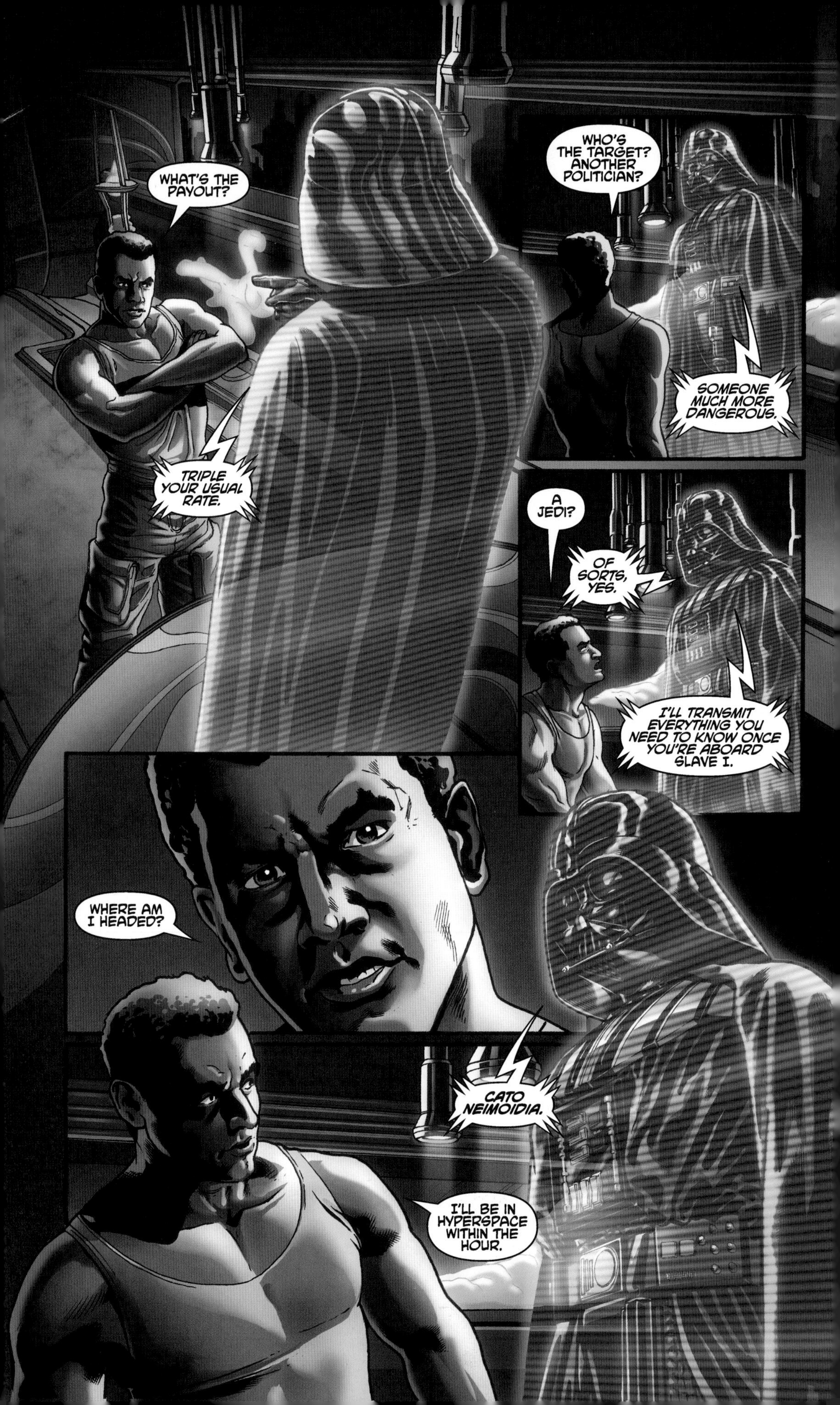
WHAT'S THE PAYOUT?
TRIPLE YOUR USUAL RATE.
WHO'S THE TARGET? ANOTHER POLITICIAN?
SOMEONE MUCH MORE DANGEROUS.
A JEDI?
OF SORTS, YES.
I'LL TRANSMIT EVERYTHING YOU NEED TO KNOW ONCE YOU'RE ABOARD SLAVE I.
WHERE AM I HEADED?
CATO NEIMOIDIA.
I'LL BE IN HYPERSPACE WITHIN THE HOUR.

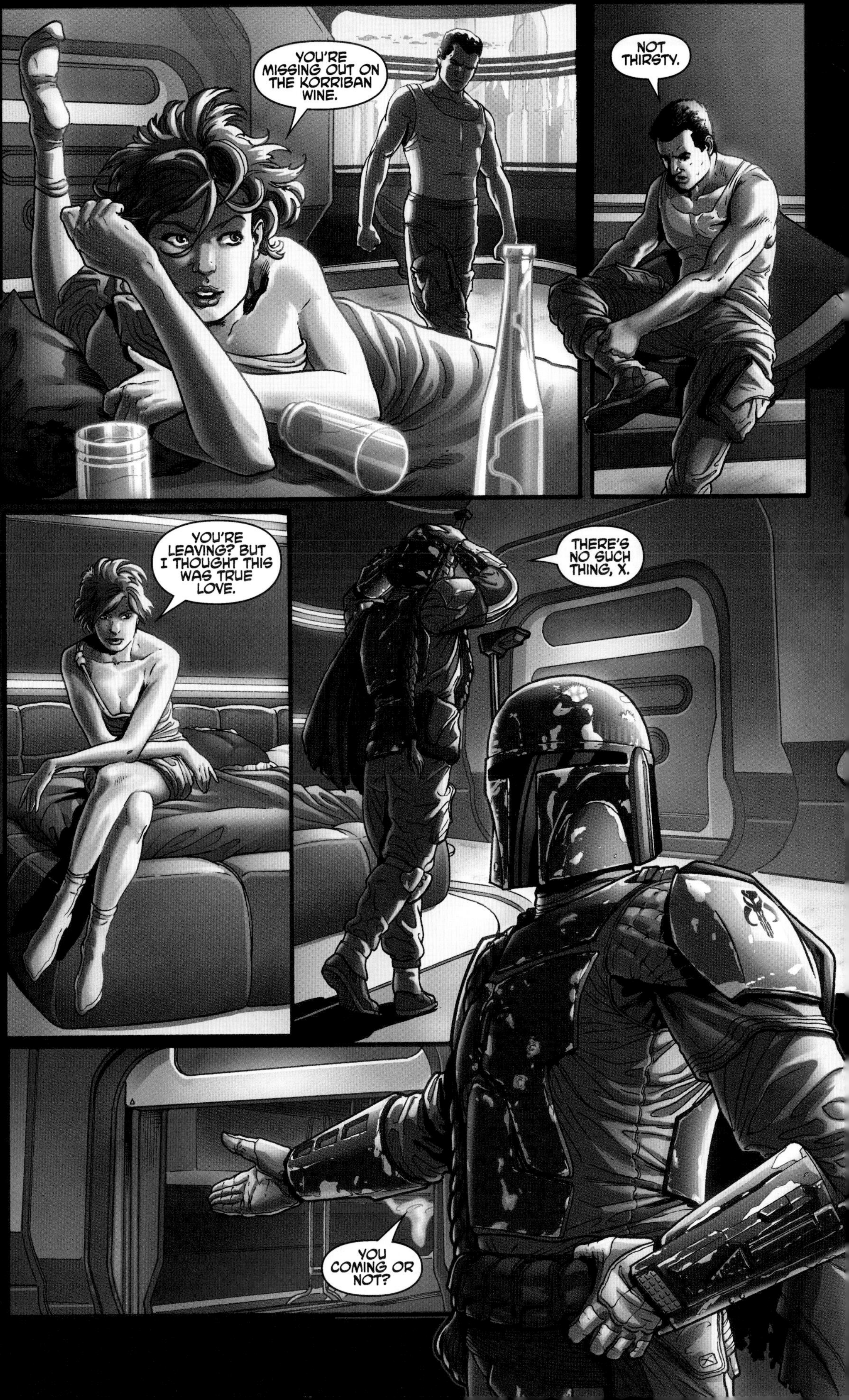
YOU'RE MISSING OUT ON THE KORRIBAN WINE.
NOT THIRSTY.
YOU'RE LEAVING? BUT I THOUGHT THIS WAS TRUE LOVE.
THERE'S NO SUCH THING, X.
YOU COMING OR NOT?

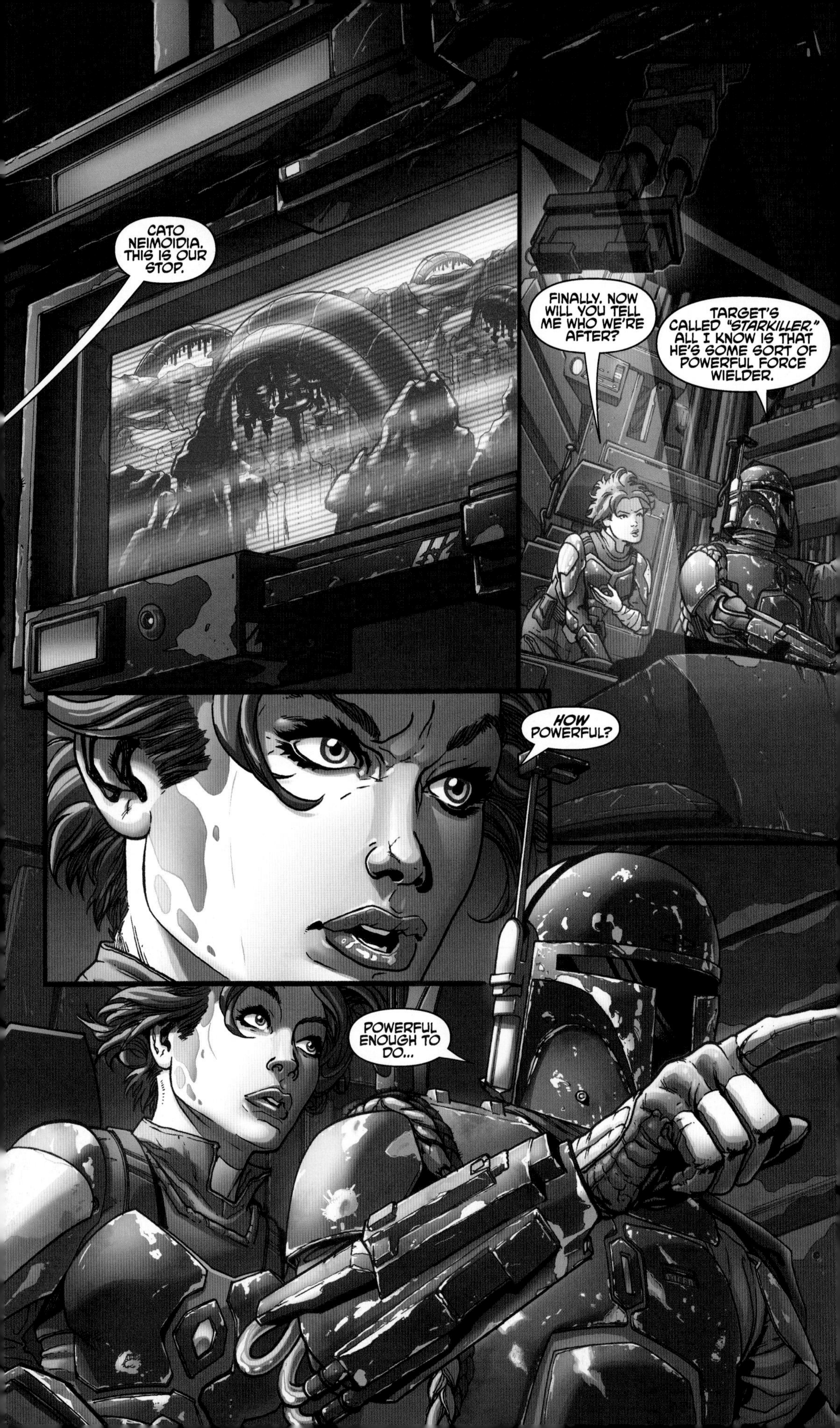
CATO NEIMOIDIA. THIS IS OUR STOP.
FINALLY. NOW WILL YOU TELL ME WHO WE'RE AFTER?
TARGET'S CALLED "STARKILLER." ALL I KNOW IS THAT HE'S SOME SORT OF POWERFUL FORCE WIELDER.
HOW POWERFUL?
POWERFUL ENOUGH TO DO...

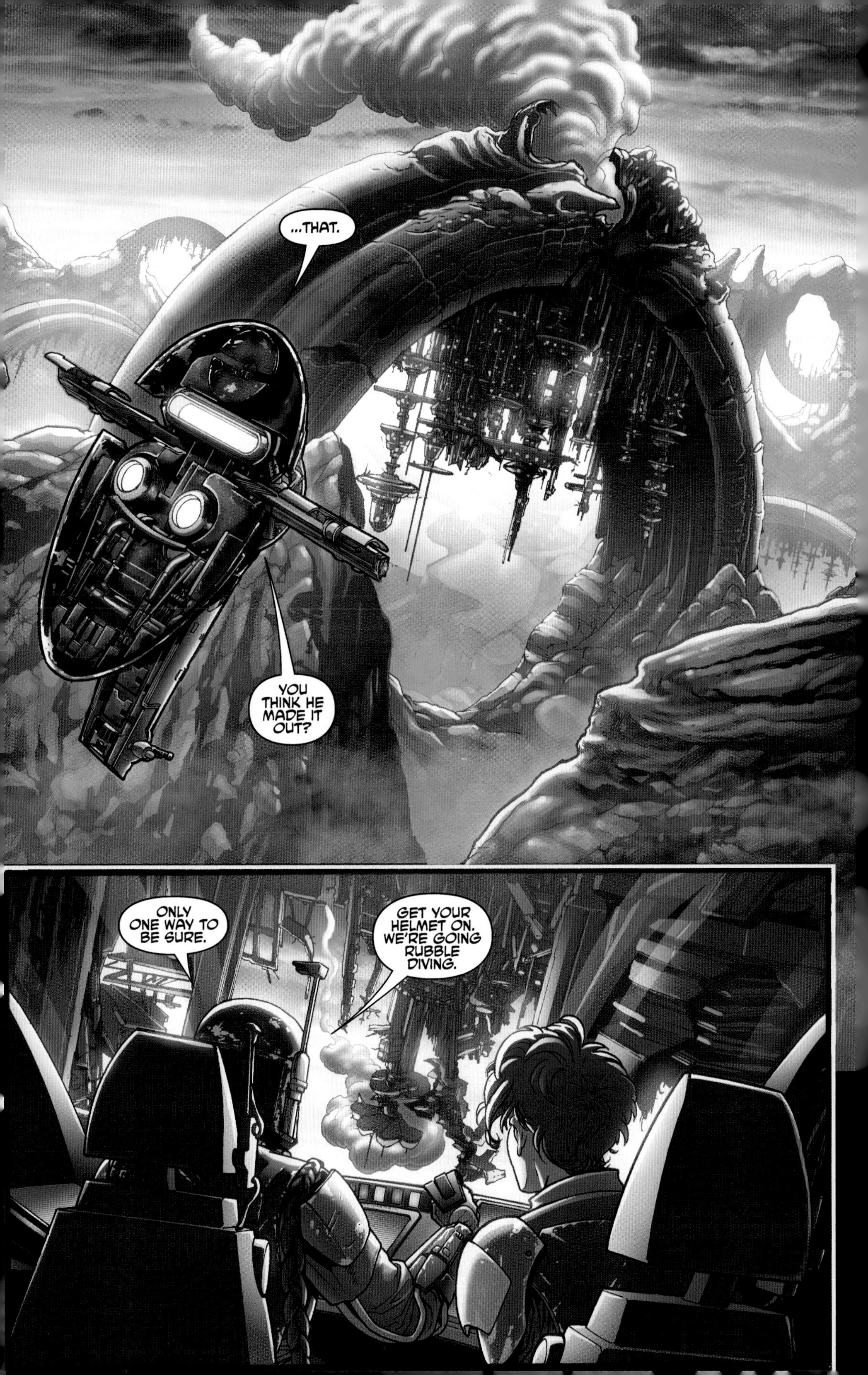
...THAT.
YOU THINK HE MADE IT OUT?
ONLY ONE WAY TO BE SURE.
GET YOUR HELMET ON. WE'RE GOING RUBBLE DIVING.

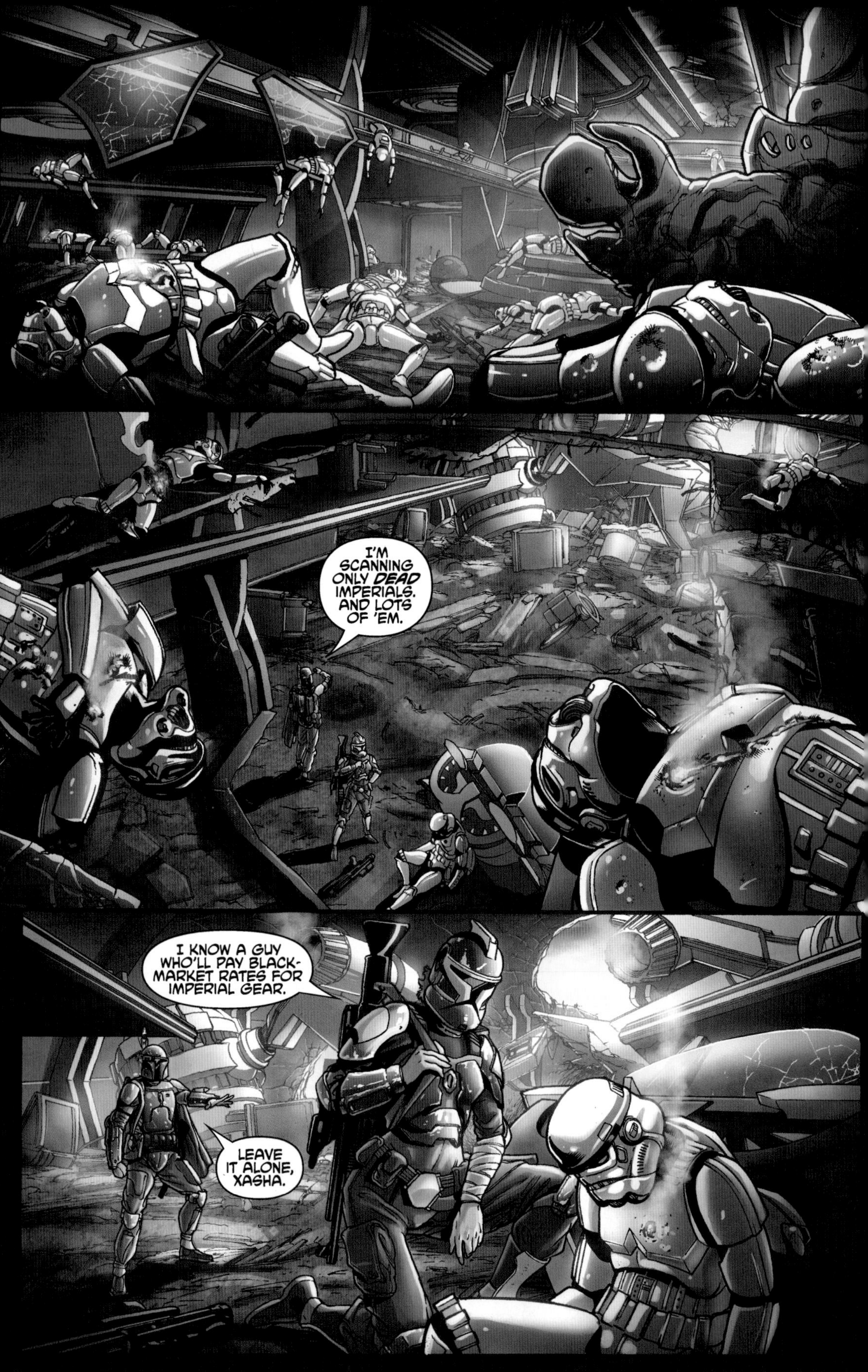

I'M SCANNING ONLY *DEAD* IMPERIALS. AND LOTS OF 'EM.
I KNOW A GUY WHO'LL PAY BLACK-MARKET RATES FOR IMPERIAL GEAR.
LEAVE IT ALONE, XASHA.

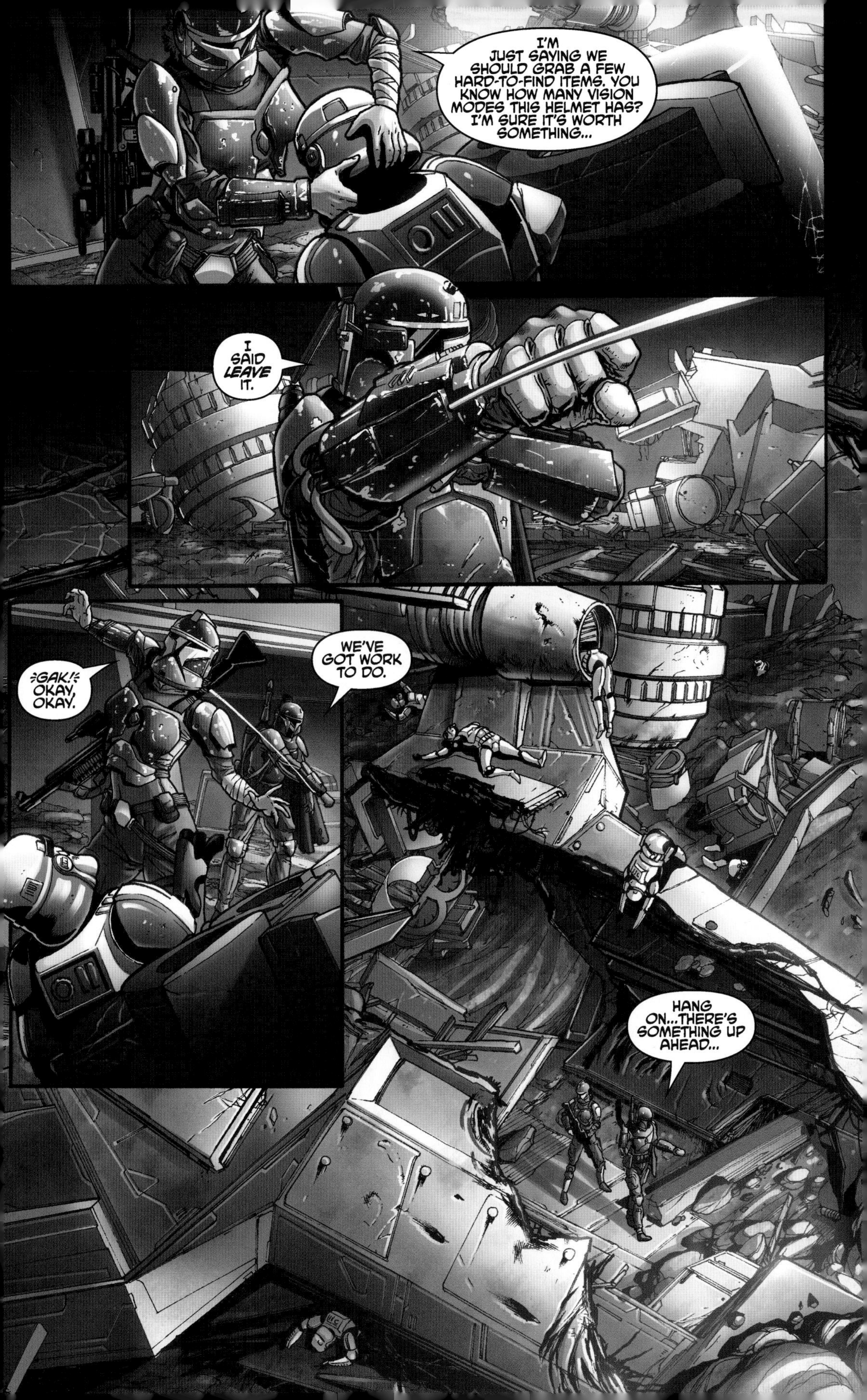
I'M JUST SAYING WE SHOULD GRAB A FEW HARD-TO-FIND ITEMS. YOU KNOW HOW MANY VISION MODES THIS HELMET HAS? I'M SURE IT'S WORTH SOMETHING...
I SAID *LEAVE* IT.
GAK! OKAY, OKAY.
WE'VE GOT WORK TO DO.
HANG ON...THERE'S SOMETHING UP AHEAD...

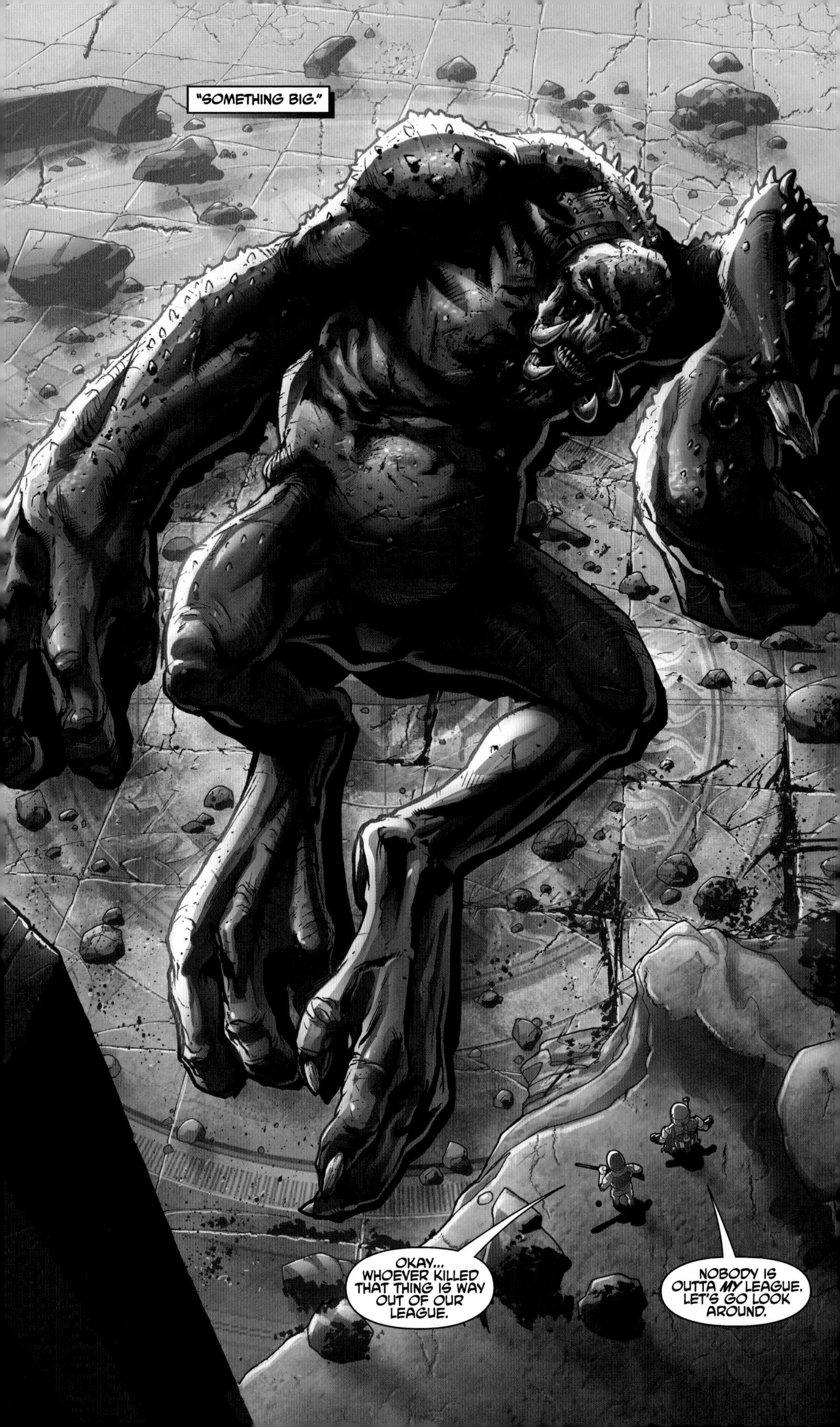
"SOMETHING BIG."
OKAY... WHOEVER KILLED THAT THING IS WAY OUT OF OUR LEAGUE.
NOBODY IS OUTTA MY LEAGUE. LET'S GO LOOK AROUND.

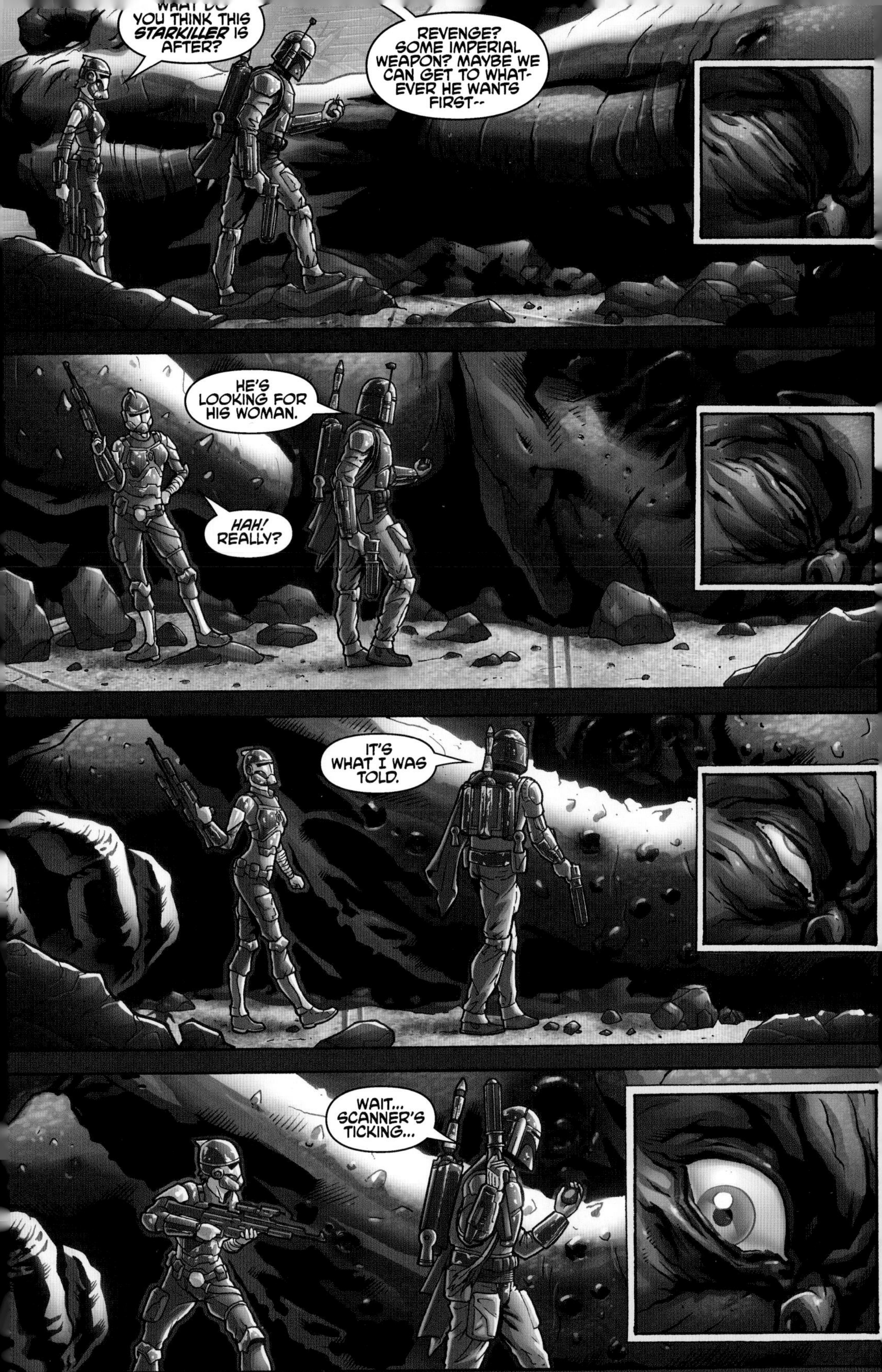
WHAT DO YOU THINK THIS *STARKILLER* IS AFTER?
REVENGE? SOME IMPERIAL WEAPON? MAYBE WE CAN GET TO WHAT-EVER HE WANTS FIRST--
HE'S LOOKING FOR HIS WOMAN.
HAH! REALLY?
IT'S WHAT I WAS TOLD.
WAIT... SCANNER'S TICKING...

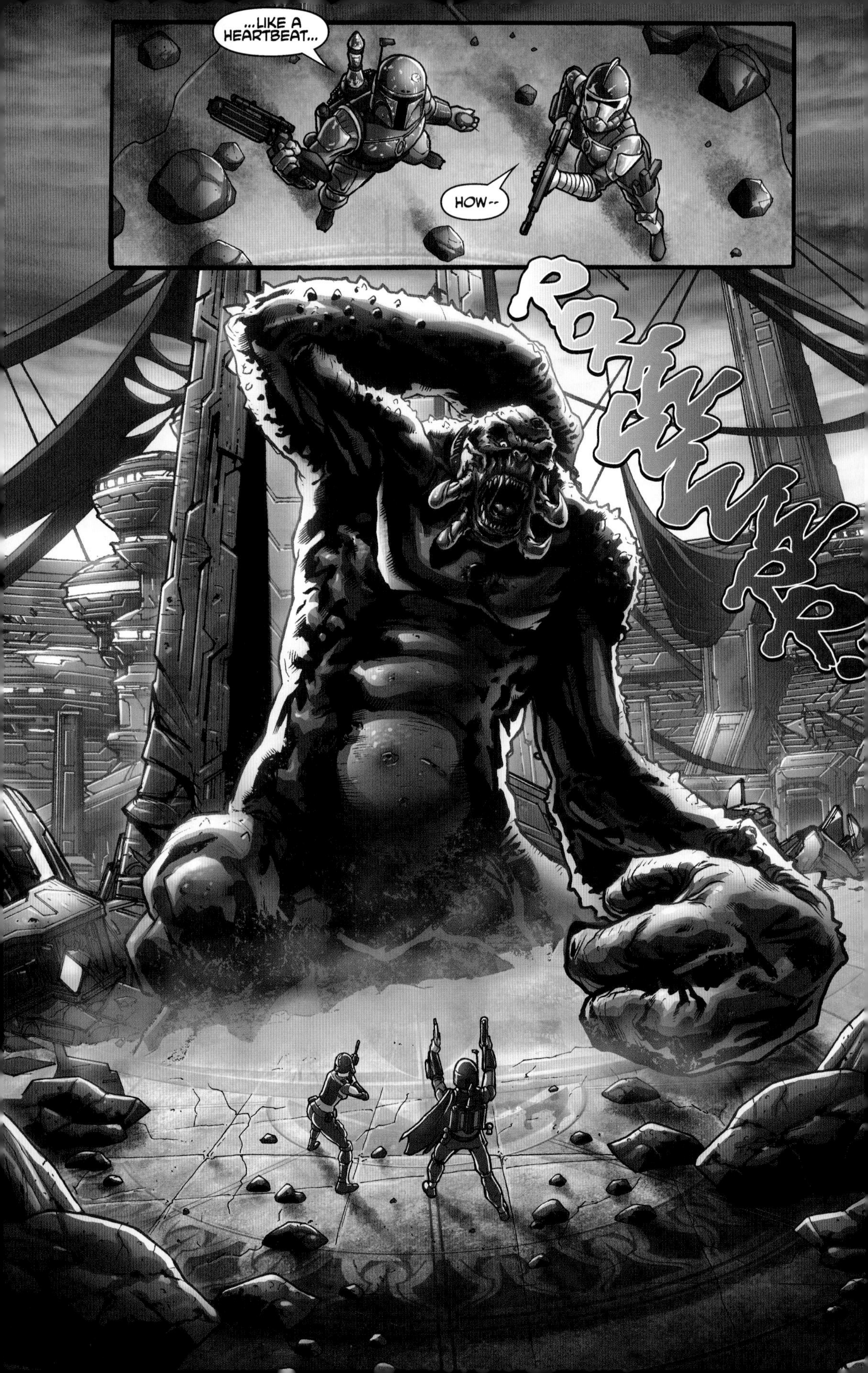
...LIKE A HEARTBEAT...
HOW--
ROAAWWRR!

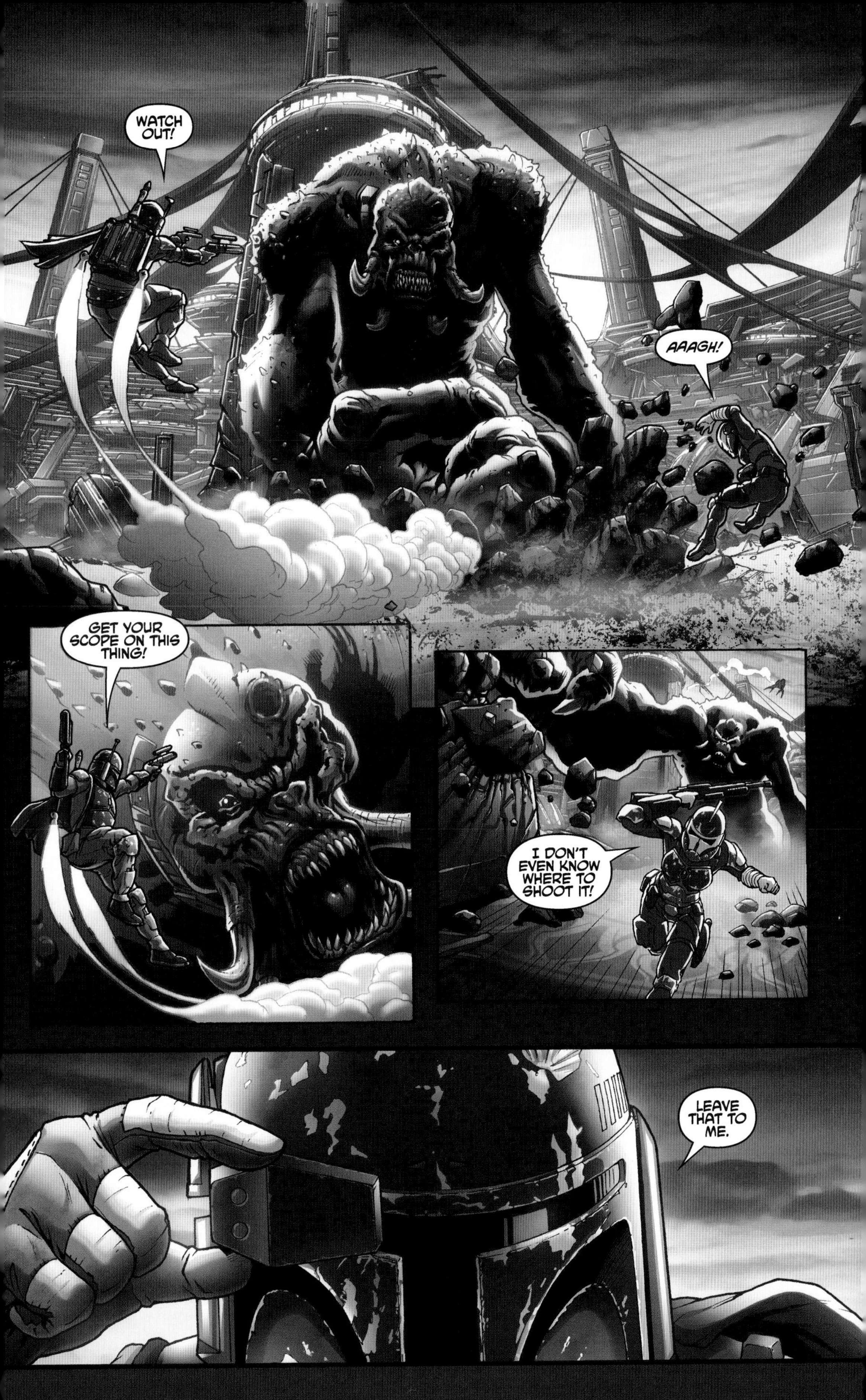
WATCH OUT!
AAAGH!
GET YOUR SCOPE ON THIS THING!
I DON'T EVEN KNOW WHERE TO SHOOT IT!
LEAVE THAT TO ME.

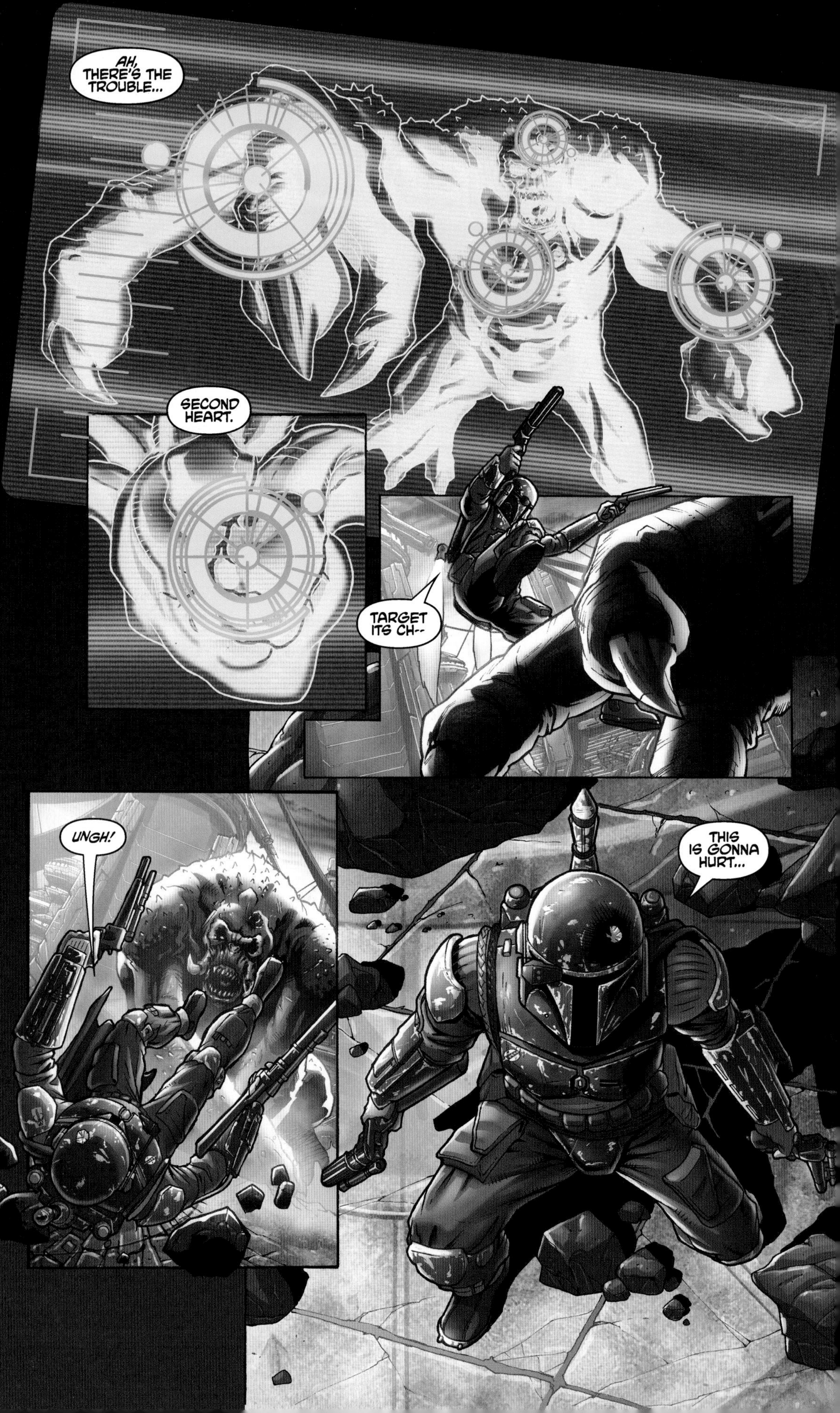
AH, THERE'S THE TROUBLE...
SECOND HEART.
TARGET ITS CH--
UNGH!
THIS IS GONNA HURT...

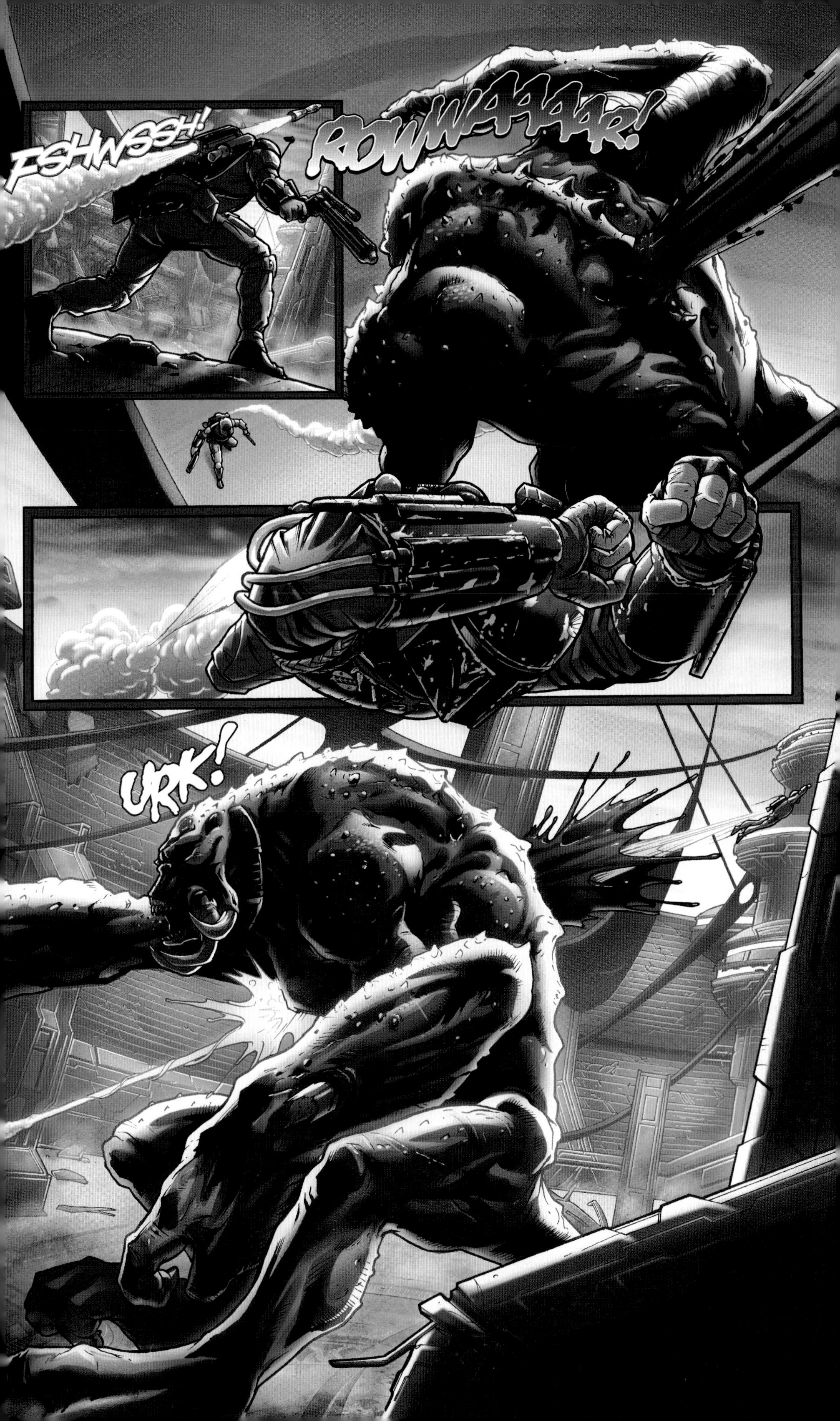
FSHWSSH!
ROWWAAAAAR!
URK!

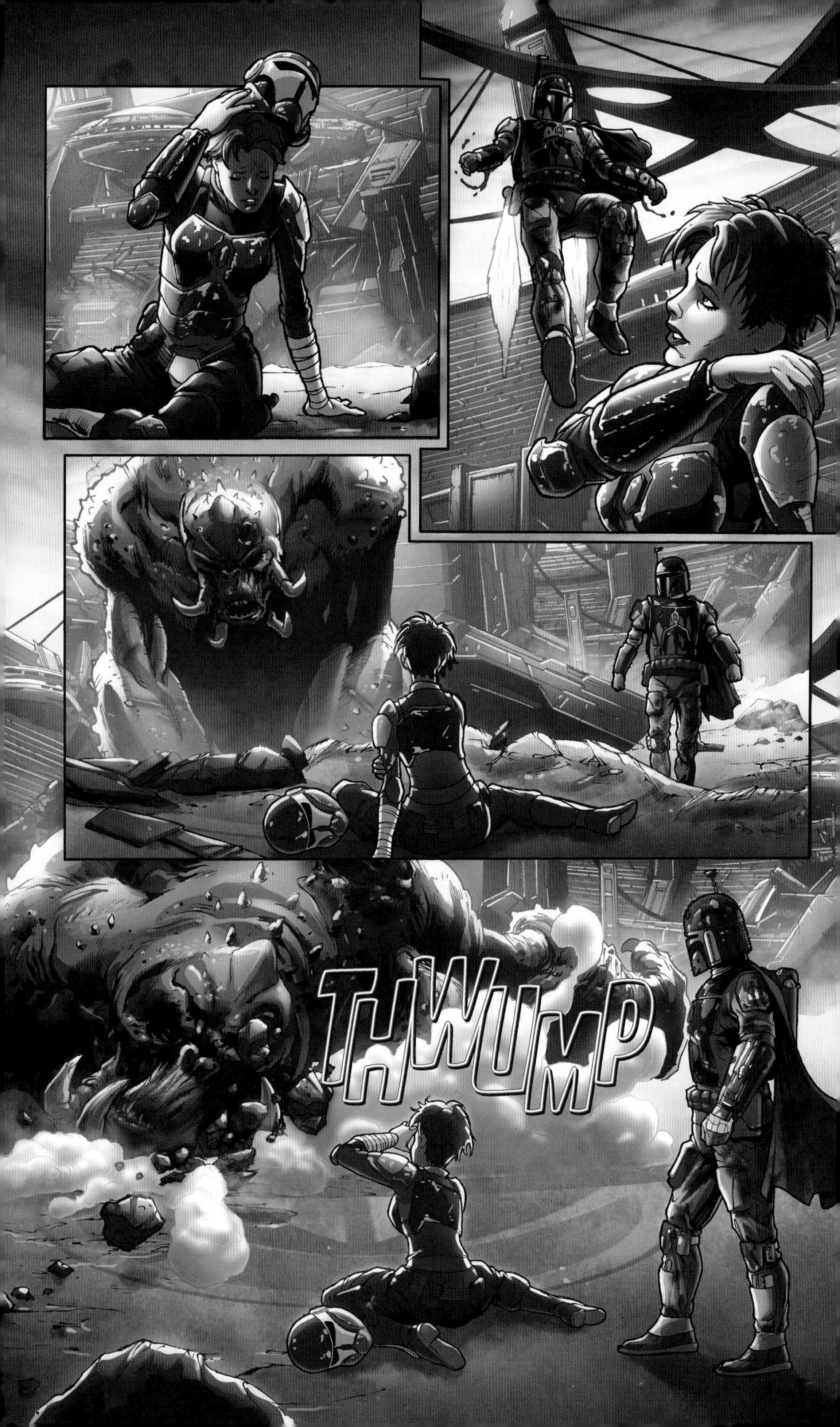
THWUMP

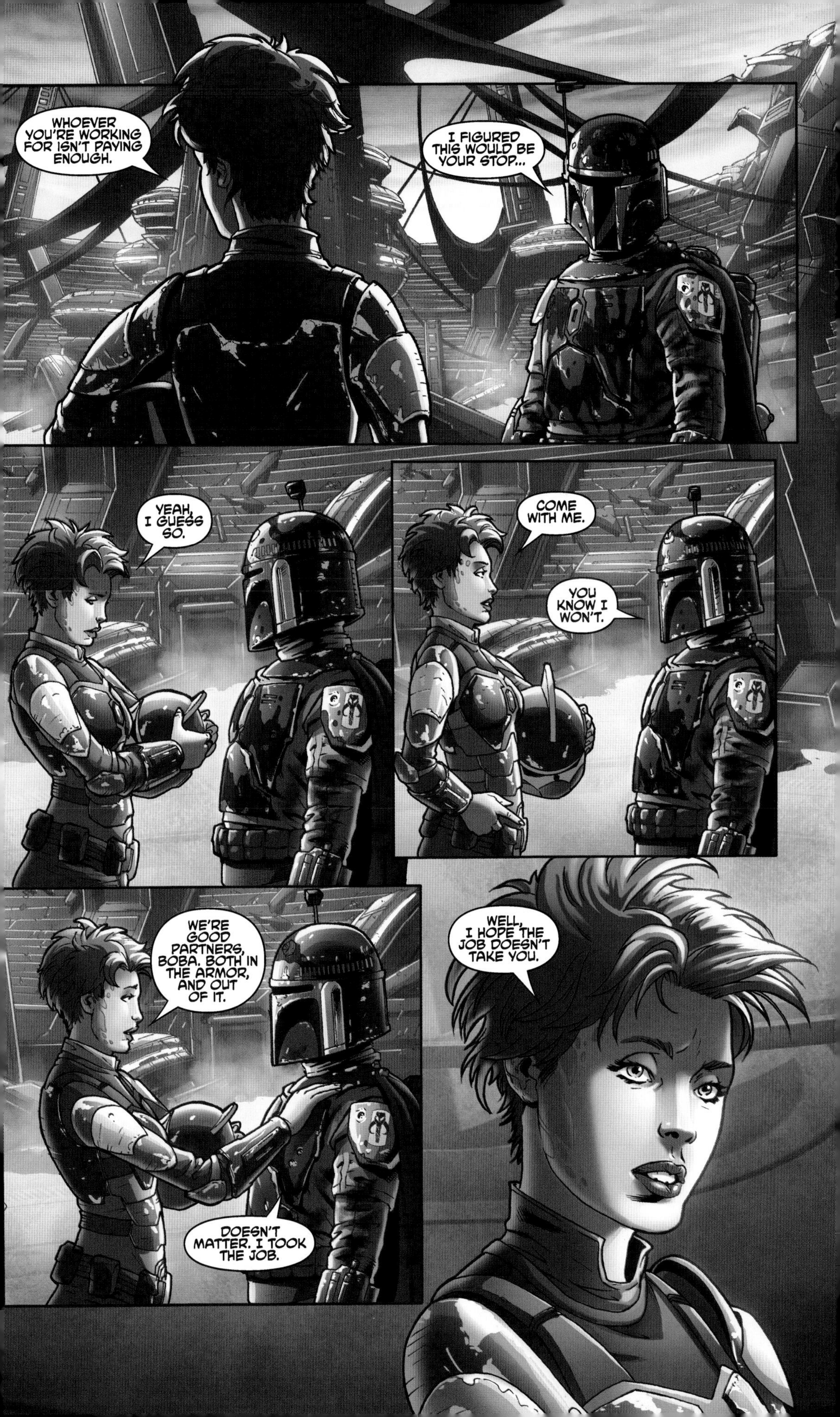
WHOEVER YOU'RE WORKING FOR ISN'T PAYING ENOUGH.
I FIGURED THIS WOULD BE YOUR STOP...
YEAH, I GUESS SO.
COME WITH ME.
YOU KNOW I WON'T.
WE'RE GOOD PARTNERS, BOBA. BOTH IN THE ARMOR, AND OUT OF IT.
DOESN'T MATTER. I TOOK THE JOB.
WELL, I HOPE THE JOB DOESN'T TAKE YOU.

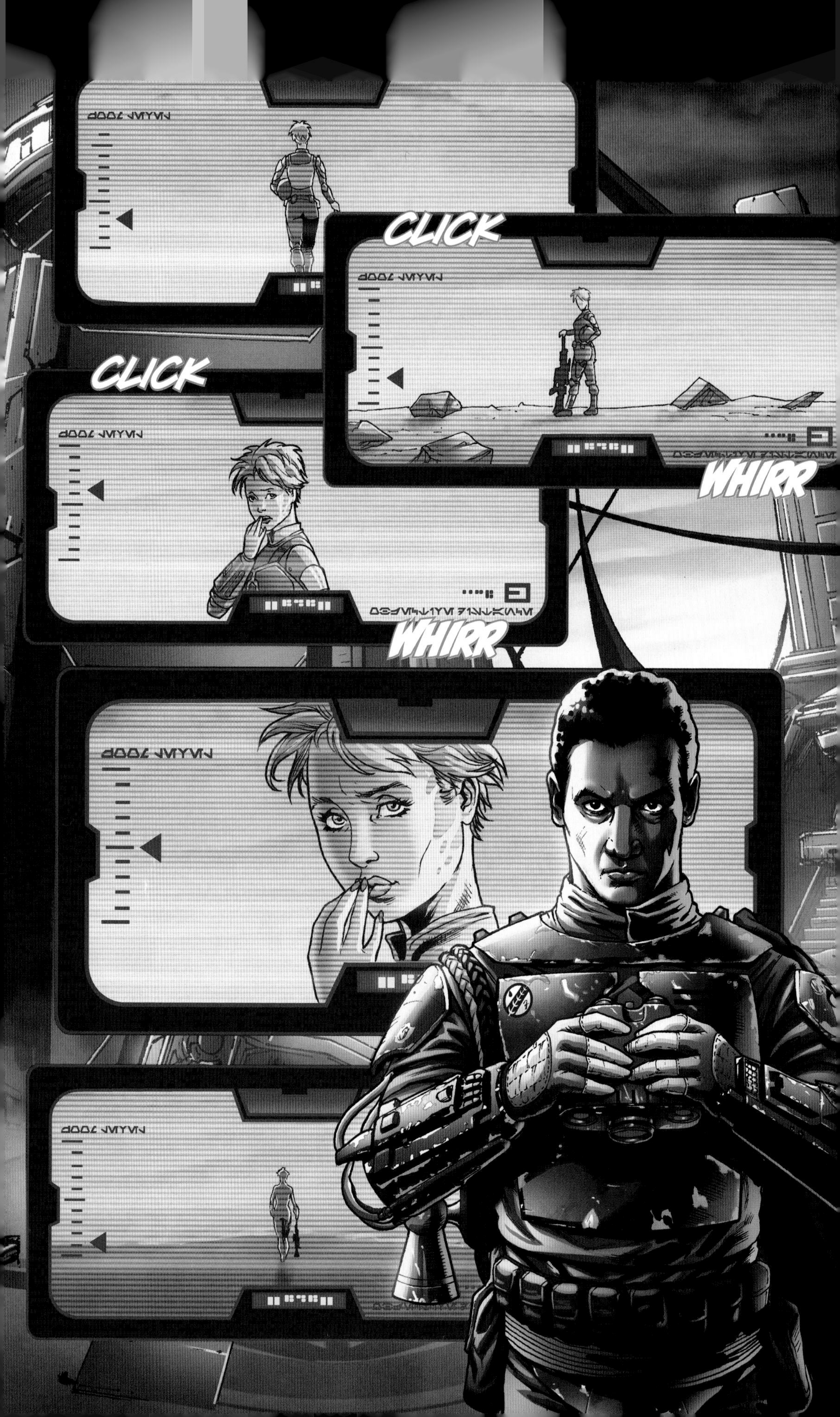
CLICK
CLICK
WHIRR
WHIRR

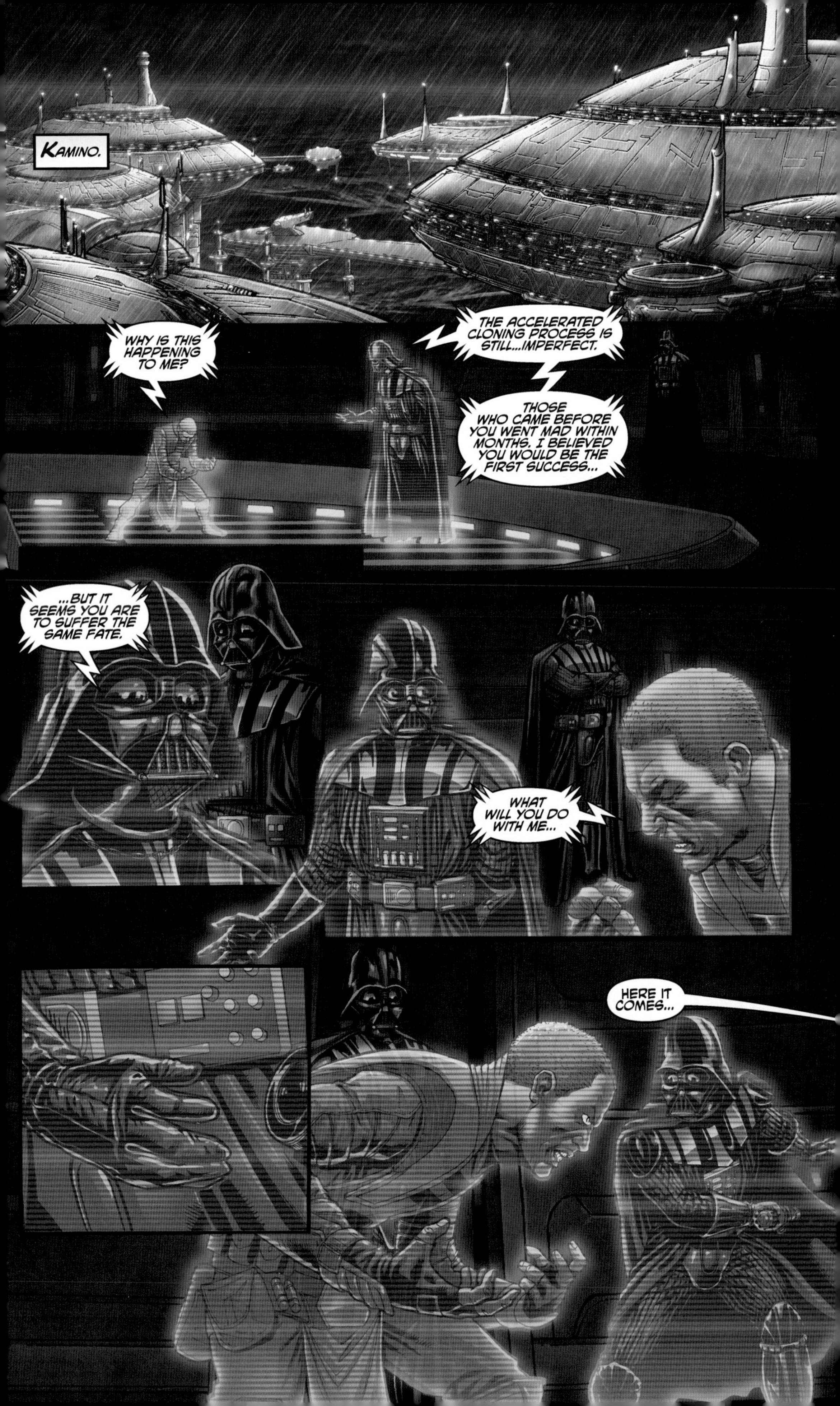
KAMINO.
WHY IS THIS HAPPENING TO ME?
THE ACCELERATED CLONING PROCESS IS STILL...IMPERFECT.
THOSE WHO CAME BEFORE YOU WENT MAD WITHIN MONTHS. I BELIEVED YOU WOULD BE THE FIRST SUCCESS...
...BUT IT SEEMS YOU ARE TO SUFFER THE SAME FATE.
WHAT WILL YOU DO WITH ME...
HERE IT COMES...

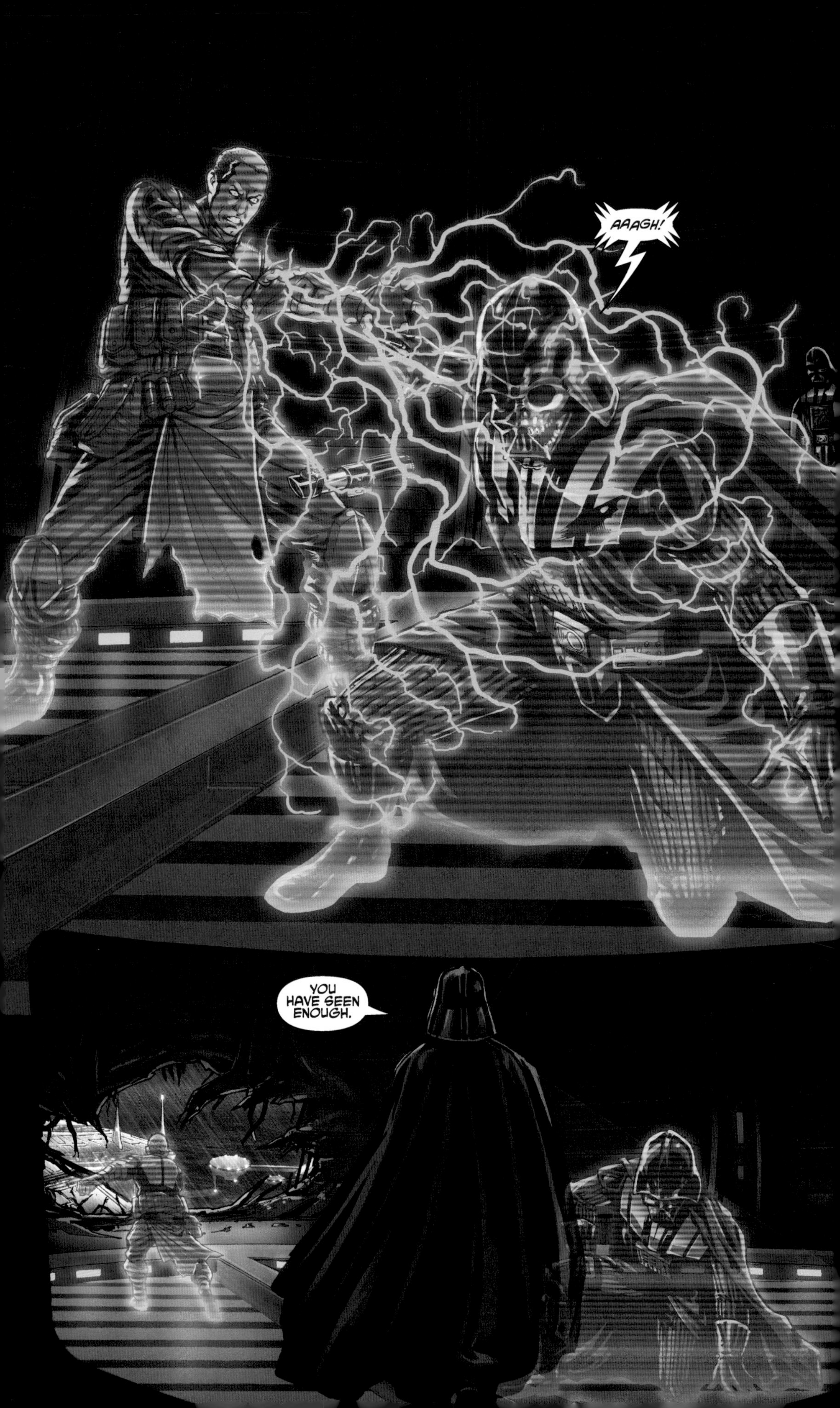
AAAGH!
YOU HAVE SEEN ENOUGH.

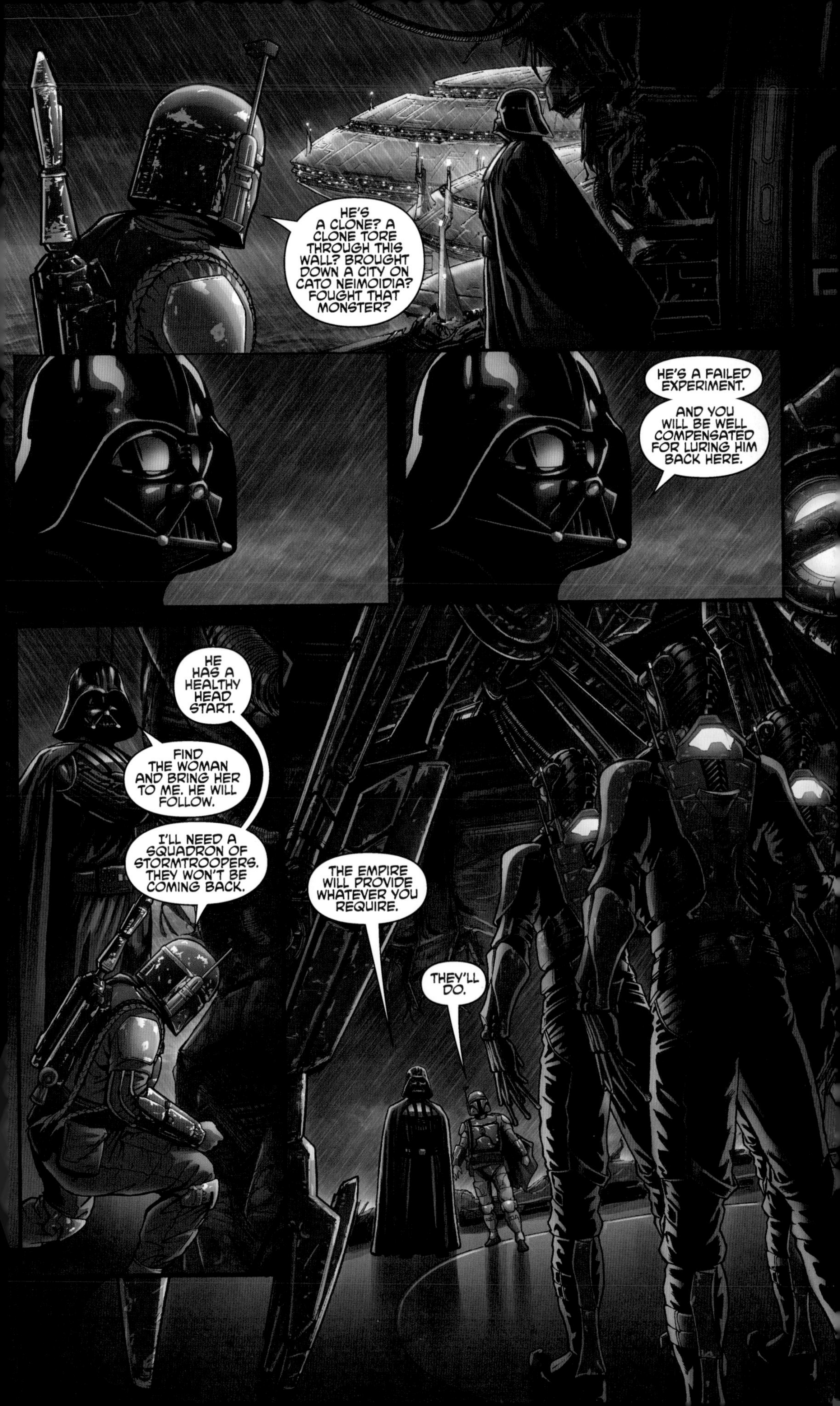
HE'S A CLONE? A CLONE TORE THROUGH THIS WALL? BROUGHT DOWN A CITY ON CATO NEIMOIDIA? FOUGHT THAT MONSTER?
HE'S A FAILED EXPERIMENT.
AND YOU WILL BE WELL COMPENSATED FOR LURING HIM BACK HERE.
HE HAS A HEALTHY HEAD START.
FIND THE WOMAN AND BRING HER TO ME. HE WILL FOLLOW.
I'LL NEED A SQUADRON OF STORMTROOPERS. THEY WON'T BE COMING BACK.
THE EMPIRE WILL PROVIDE WHATEVER YOU REQUIRE.
THEY'LL DO.

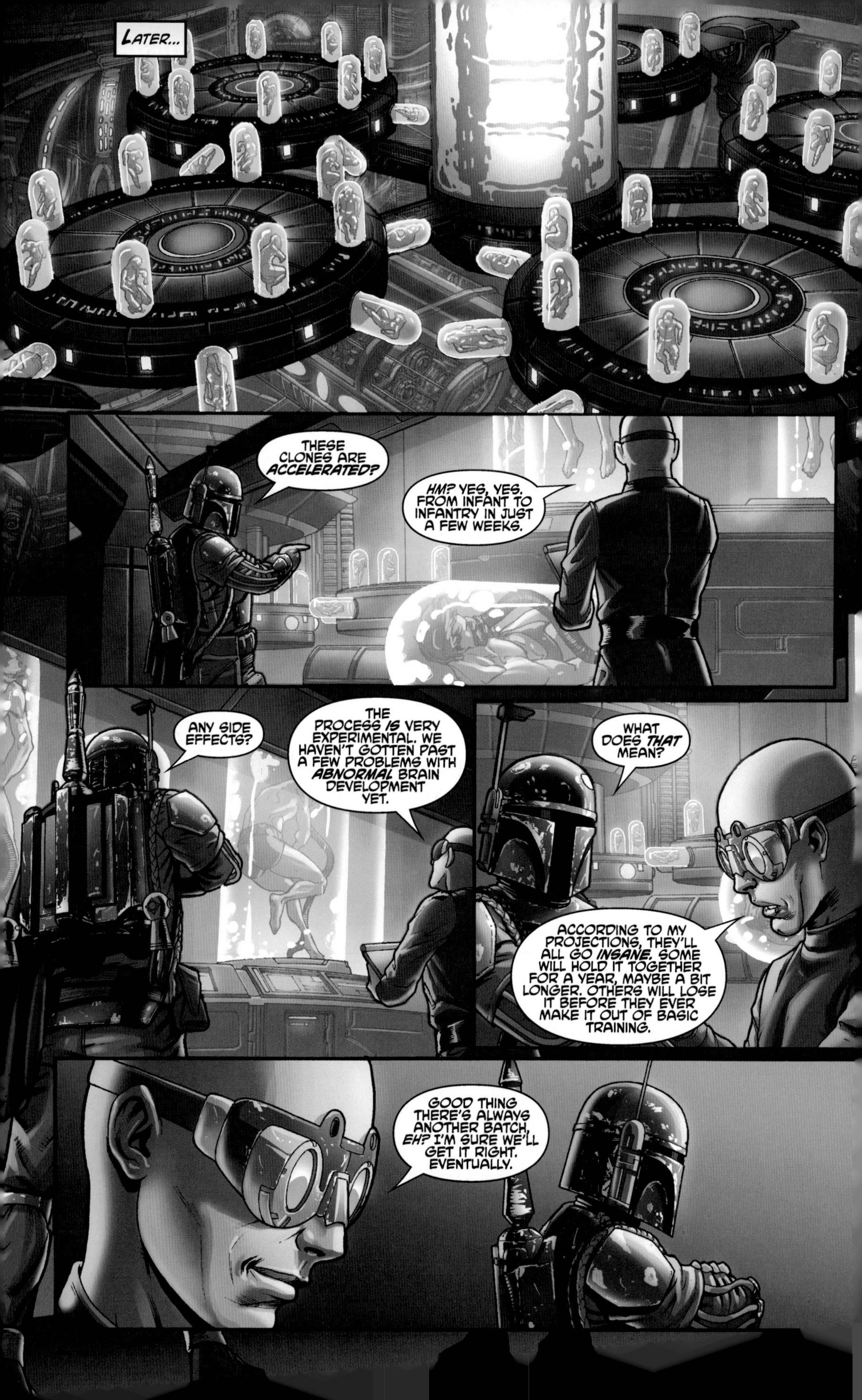
LATER...
THESE CLONES ARE ACCELERATED?
HM? YES, YES. FROM INFANT TO INFANTRY IN JUST A FEW WEEKS.
ANY SIDE EFFECTS?
THE PROCESS IS VERY EXPERIMENTAL. WE HAVEN'T GOTTEN PAST A FEW PROBLEMS WITH ABNORMAL BRAIN DEVELOPMENT YET.
WHAT DOES THAT MEAN?
ACCORDING TO MY PROJECTIONS, THEY'LL ALL GO INSANE. SOME WILL HOLD IT TOGETHER FOR A YEAR, MAYBE A BIT LONGER. OTHERS WILL LOSE IT BEFORE THEY EVER MAKE IT OUT OF BASIC TRAINING.
GOOD THING THERE'S ALWAYS ANOTHER BATCH, EH? I'M SURE WE'LL GET IT RIGHT. EVENTUALLY.

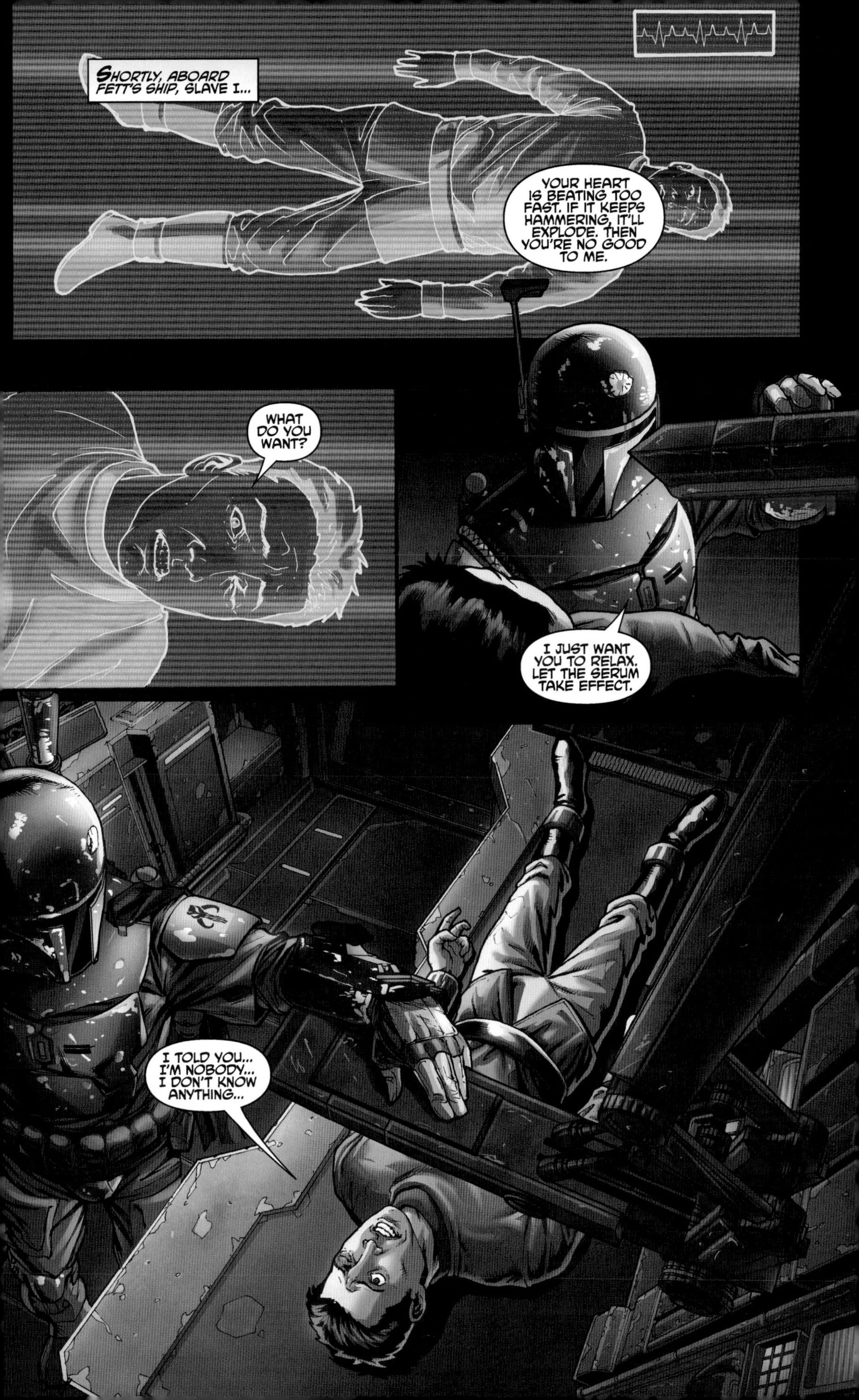
SHORTLY, ABOARD FETT'S SHIP, SLAVE I...
YOUR HEART IS BEATING TOO FAST. IF IT KEEPS HAMMERING, IT'LL EXPLODE. THEN YOU'RE NO GOOD TO ME.
WHAT DO YOU WANT?
I JUST WANT YOU TO RELAX. LET THE SERUM TAKE EFFECT.
I TOLD YOU... I'M NOBODY... I DON'T KNOW ANYTHING...

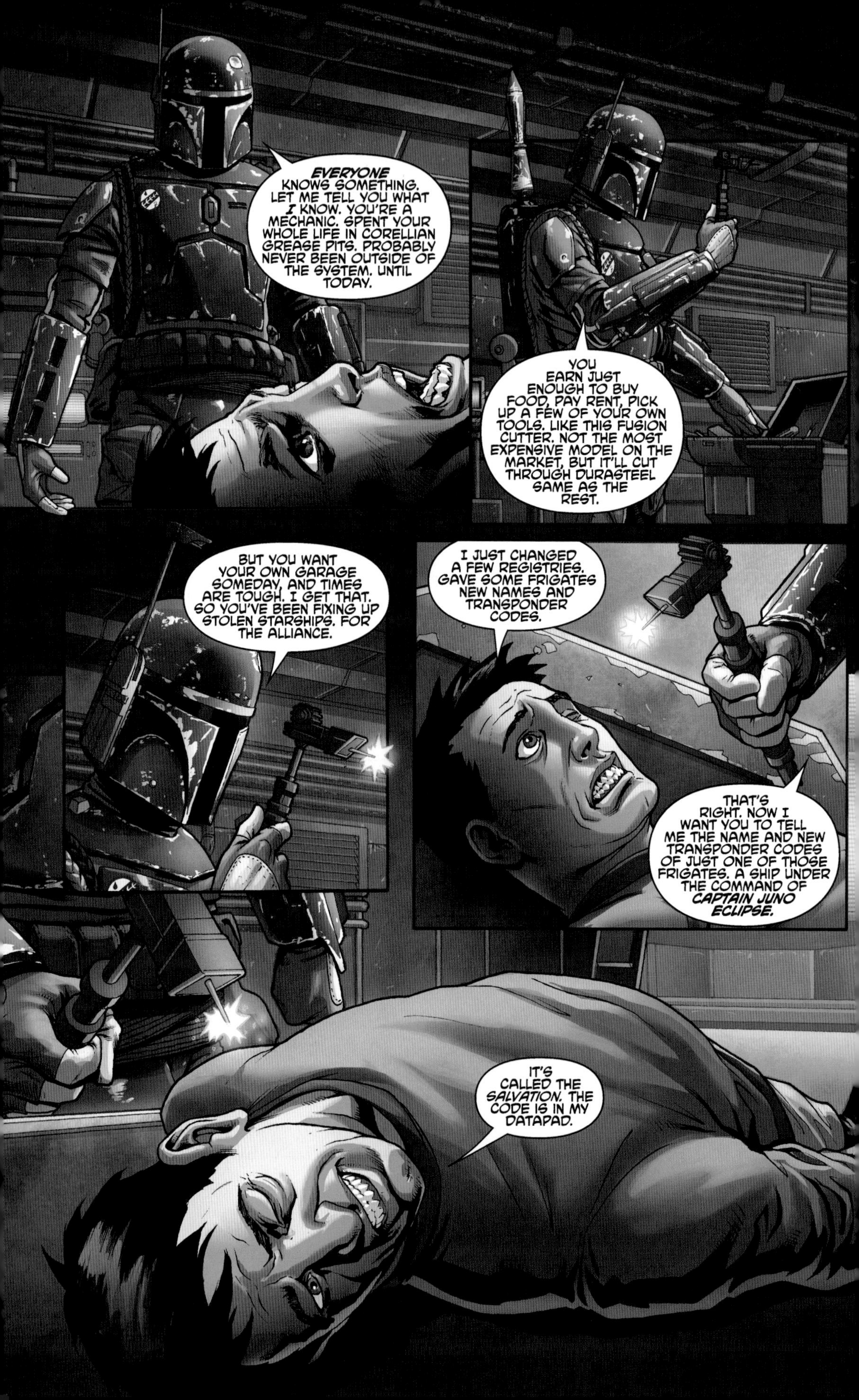
EVERYONE KNOWS SOMETHING. LET ME TELL YOU WHAT I KNOW. YOU'RE A MECHANIC. SPENT YOUR WHOLE LIFE IN CORELLIAN GREASE PITS. PROBABLY NEVER BEEN OUTSIDE OF THE SYSTEM. UNTIL TODAY.
YOU EARN JUST ENOUGH TO BUY FOOD, PAY RENT, PICK UP A FEW OF YOUR OWN TOOLS. LIKE THIS FUSION CUTTER. NOT THE MOST EXPENSIVE MODEL ON THE MARKET, BUT IT'LL CUT THROUGH DURASTEEL SAME AS THE REST.
BUT YOU WANT YOUR OWN GARAGE SOMEDAY, AND TIMES ARE TOUGH. I GET THAT. SO YOU'VE BEEN FIXING UP STOLEN STARSHIPS. FOR THE ALLIANCE.
I JUST CHANGED A FEW REGISTRIES. GAVE SOME FRIGATES NEW NAMES AND TRANSPONDER CODES.
THAT'S RIGHT. NOW I WANT YOU TO TELL ME THE NAME AND NEW TRANSPONDER CODES OF JUST ONE OF THOSE FRIGATES. A SHIP UNDER THE COMMAND OF CAPTAIN JUNO ECLIPSE.
IT'S CALLED THE SALVATION. THE CODE IS IN MY DATAPAD.

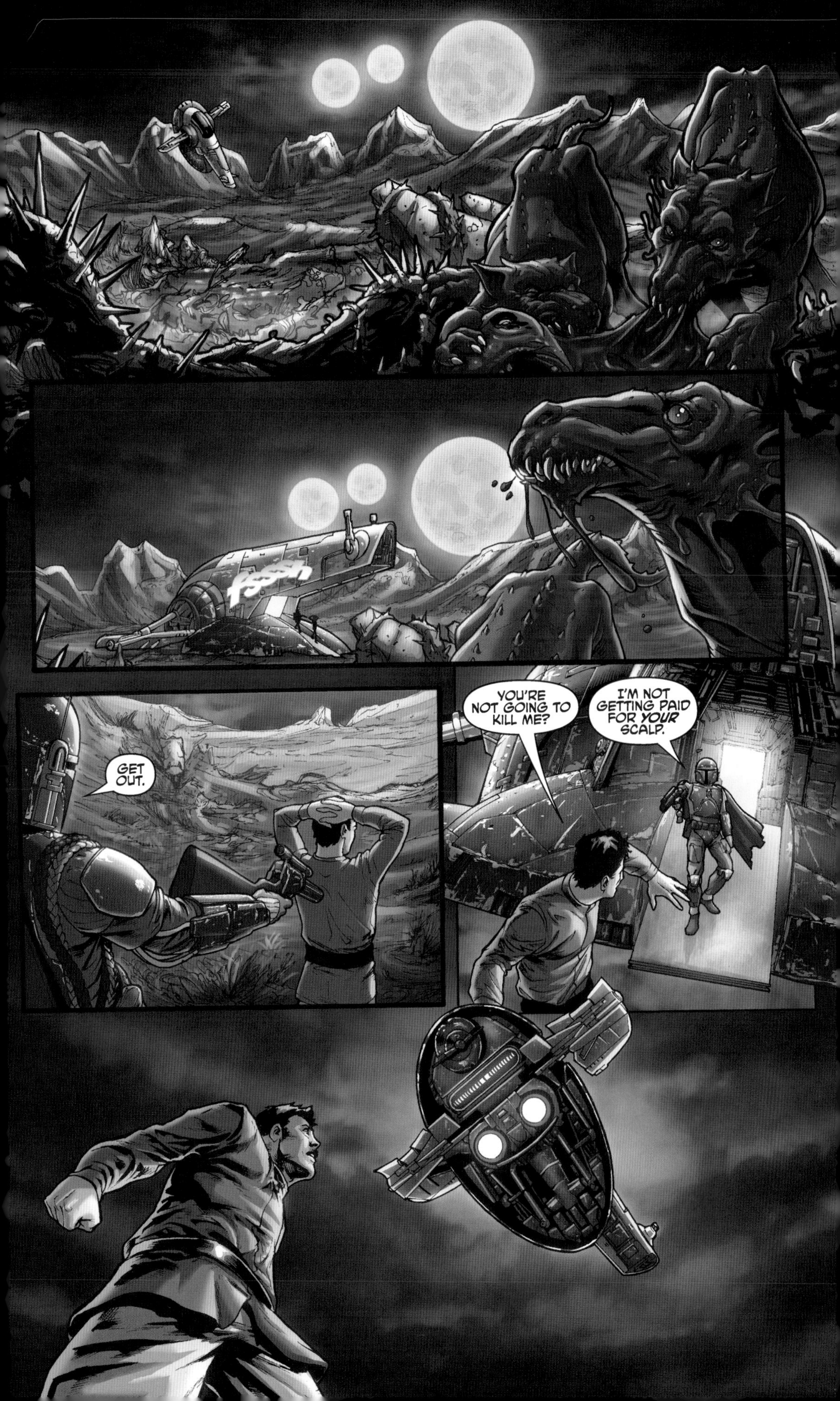
FSSH
GET OUT.
YOU'RE NOT GOING TO KILL ME?
I'M NOT GETTING PAID FOR *YOUR* SCALP.

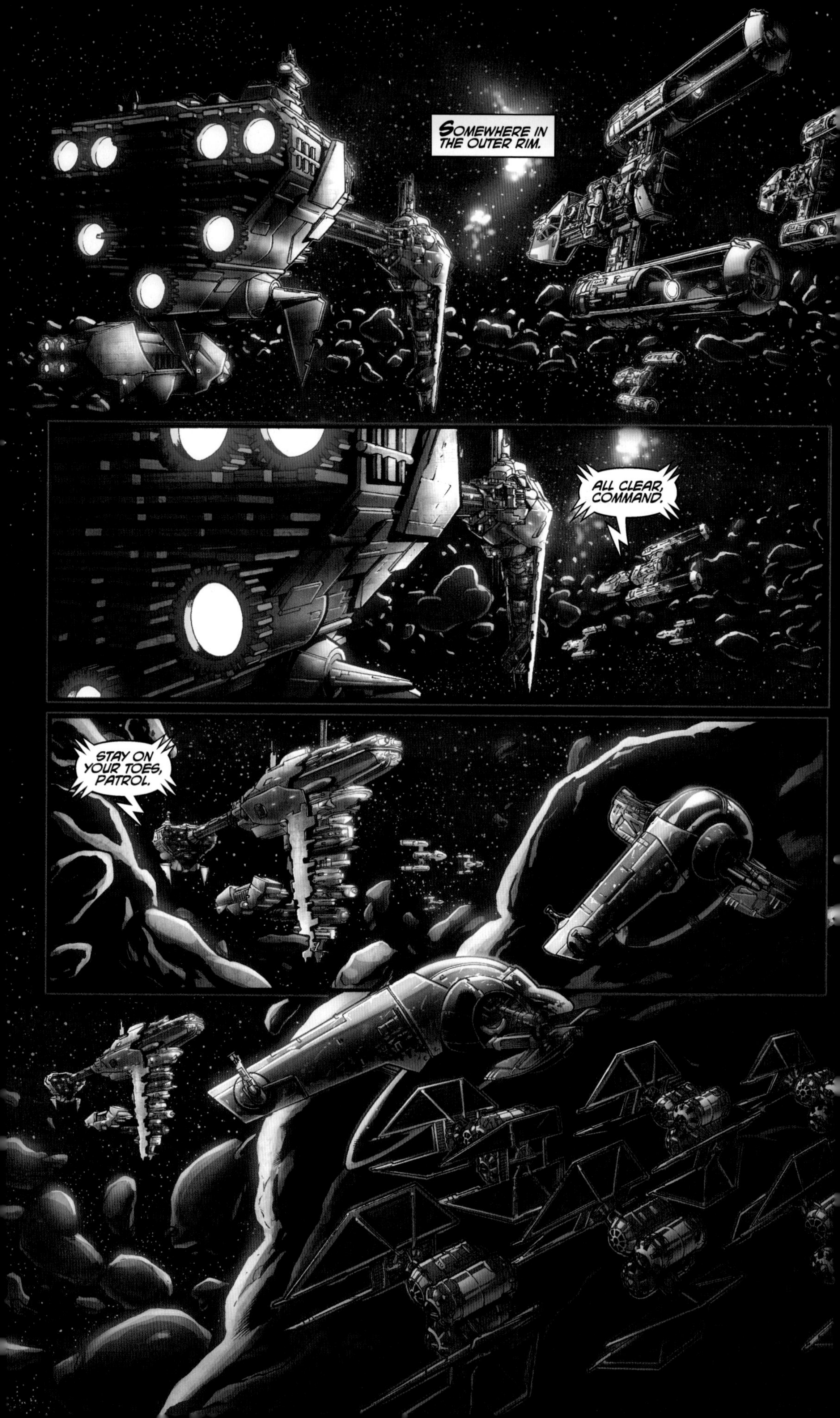
SOMEWHERE IN THE OUTER RIM.
ALL CLEAR, COMMAND.
STAY ON YOUR TOES, PATROL.

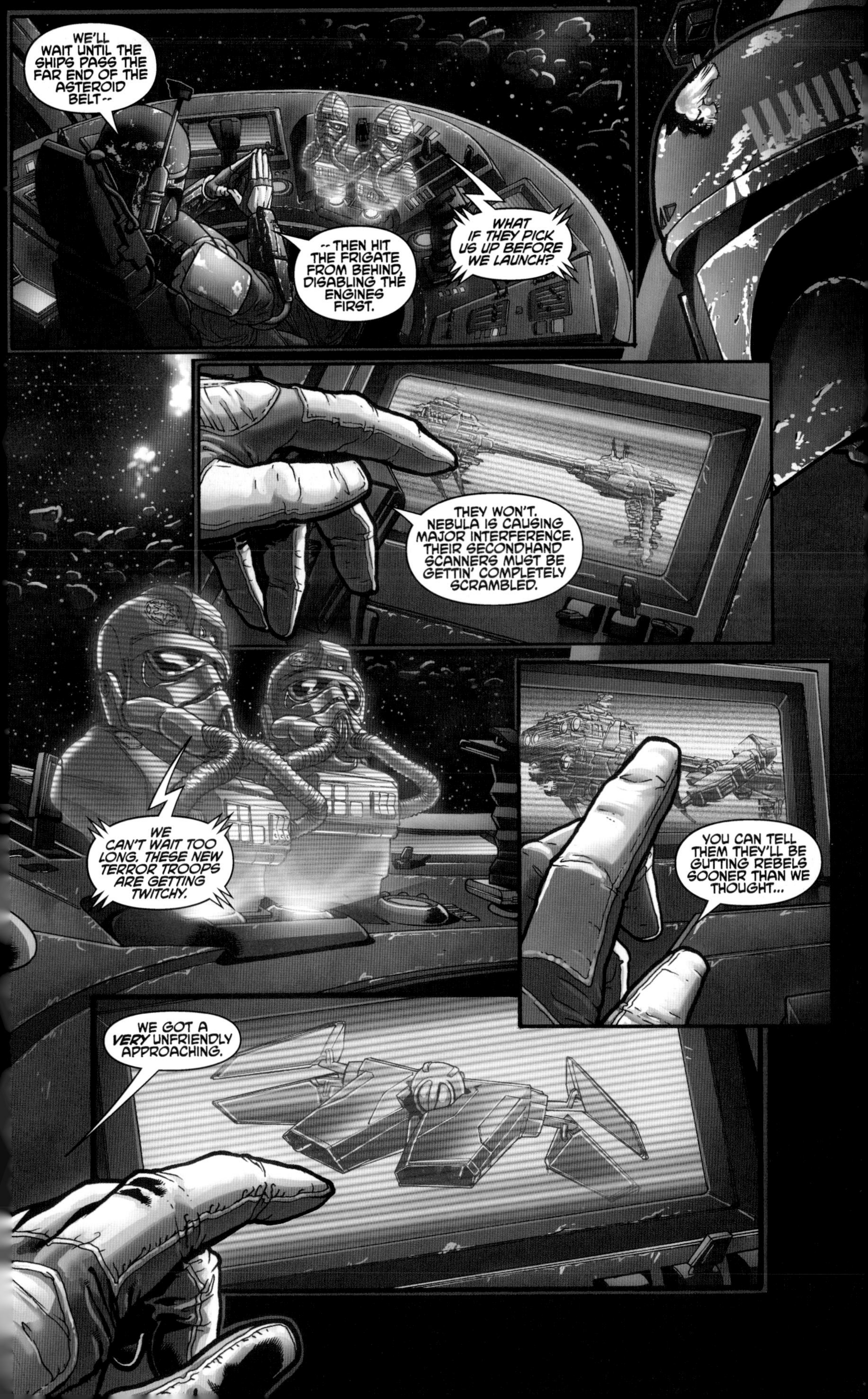
WE'LL WAIT UNTIL THE SHIPS PASS THE FAR END OF THE ASTEROID BELT--
--THEN HIT THE FRIGATE FROM BEHIND, DISABLING THE ENGINES FIRST.
WHAT IF THEY PICK US UP BEFORE WE LAUNCH?
THEY WON'T. NEBULA IS CAUSING MAJOR INTERFERENCE. THEIR SECONDHAND SCANNERS MUST BE GETTIN' COMPLETELY SCRAMBLED.
WE CAN'T WAIT TOO LONG. THESE NEW TERROR TROOPS ARE GETTING TWITCHY.
YOU CAN TELL THEM THEY'LL BE GUTTING REBELS SOONER THAN WE THOUGHT...
WE GOT A VERY UNFRIENDLY APPROACHING.

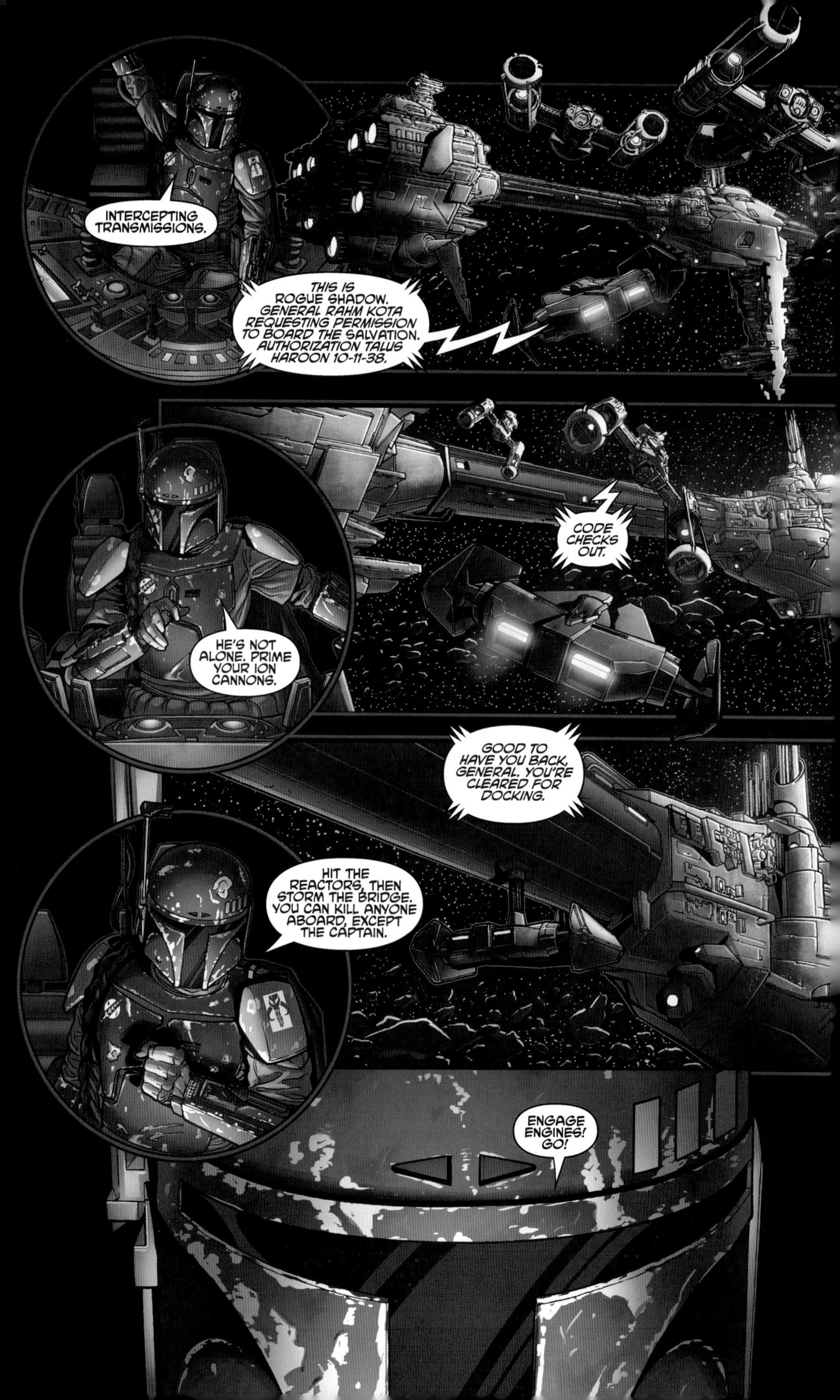
INTERCEPTING TRANSMISSIONS.
THIS IS ROGUE SHADOW. GENERAL RAHM KOTA REQUESTING PERMISSION TO BOARD THE SALVATION. AUTHORIZATION TALUS HAROON 10-11-38.
CODE CHECKS OUT.
HE'S NOT ALONE. PRIME YOUR ION CANNONS.
GOOD TO HAVE YOU BACK, GENERAL. YOU'RE CLEARED FOR DOCKING.
HIT THE REACTORS, THEN STORM THE BRIDGE. YOU CAN KILL ANYONE ABOARD, EXCEPT THE CAPTAIN.
ENGAGE ENGINES! GO!

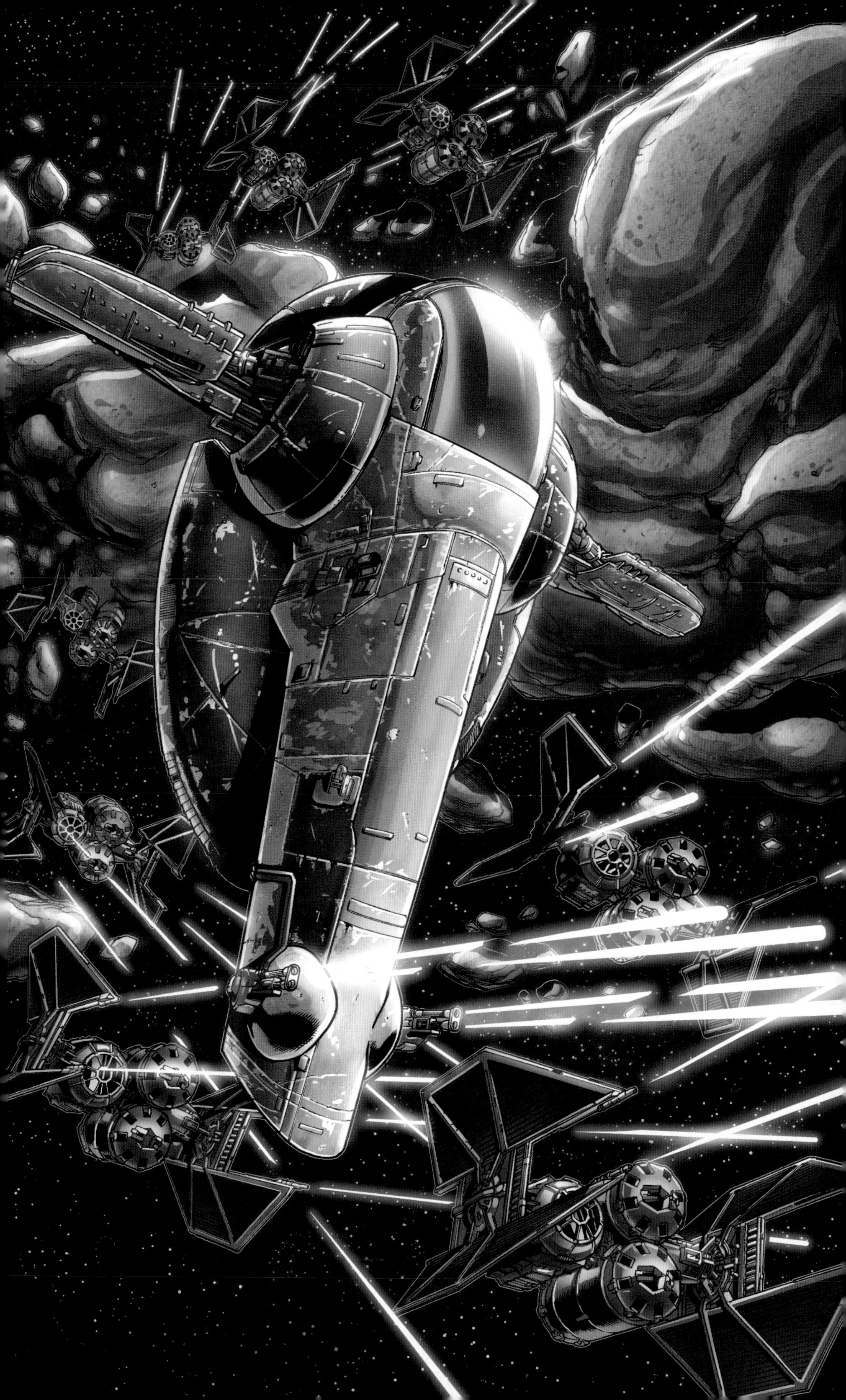

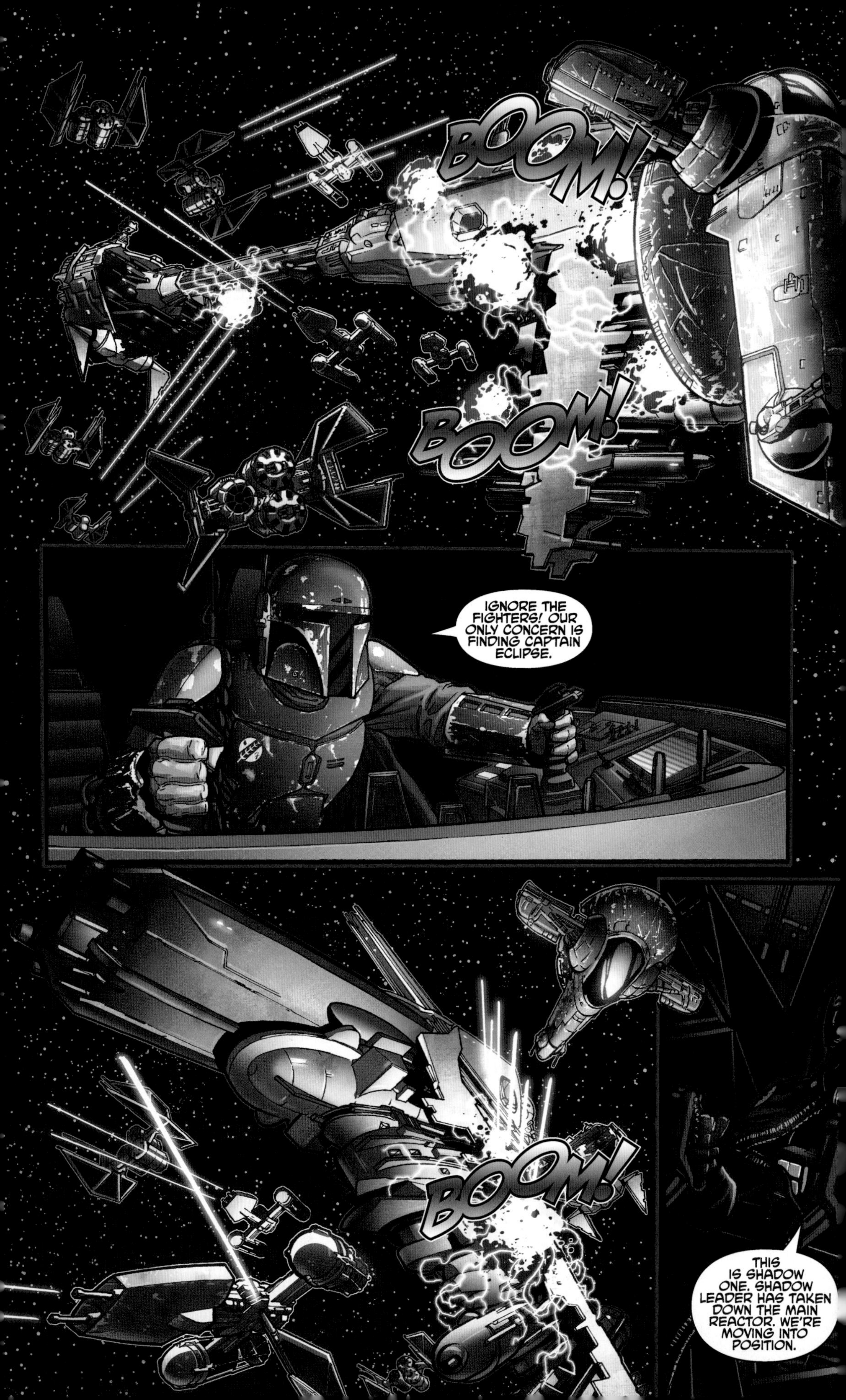
BOOM!
BOOM!
IGNORE THE FIGHTERS! OUR ONLY CONCERN IS FINDING CAPTAIN ECLIPSE.
BOOM!
THIS IS SHADOW ONE. SHADOW LEADER HAS TAKEN DOWN THE MAIN REACTOR. WE'RE MOVING INTO POSITION.

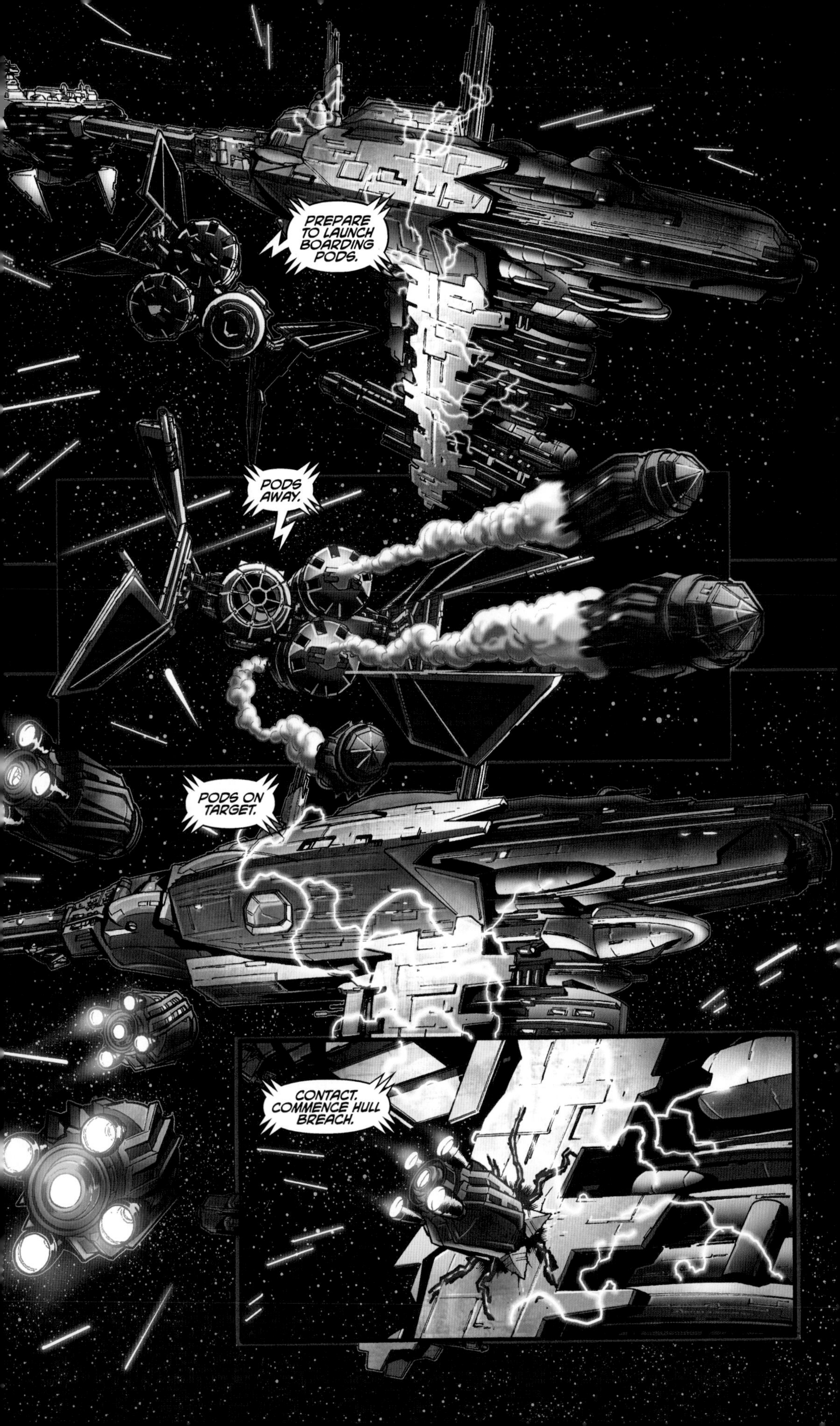
PREPARE TO LAUNCH BOARDING PODS.
PODS AWAY.
PODS ON TARGET.
CONTACT. COMMENCE HULL BREACH.

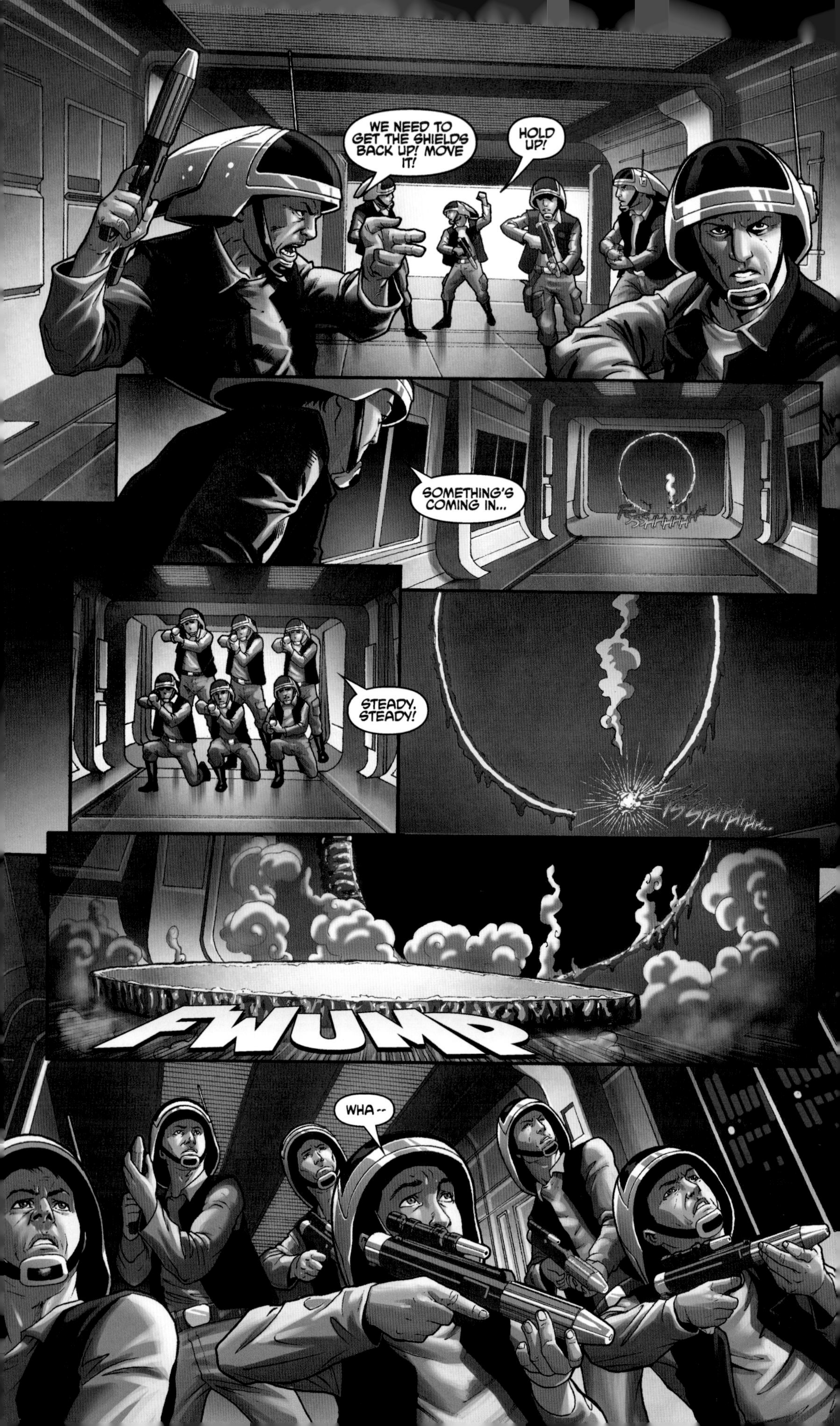
WE NEED TO GET THE SHIELDS BACK UP! MOVE IT!
HOLD UP!
SOMETHING'S COMING IN...
FSSHHHHHH
STEADY. STEADY!
FSSHHHH...
FWUMP
WHA --

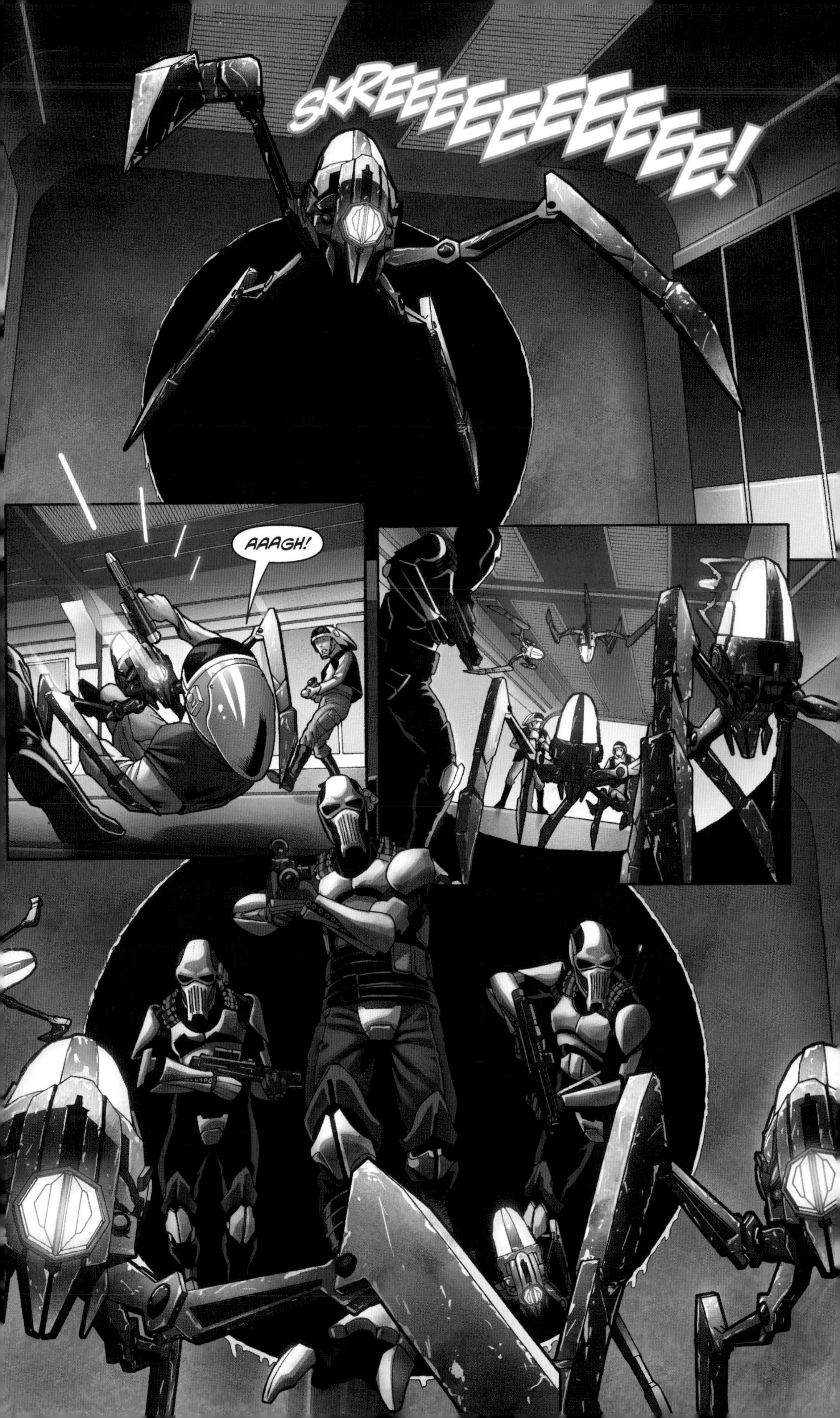
SKREEEEEEEEEEEEE!
AAAGH!

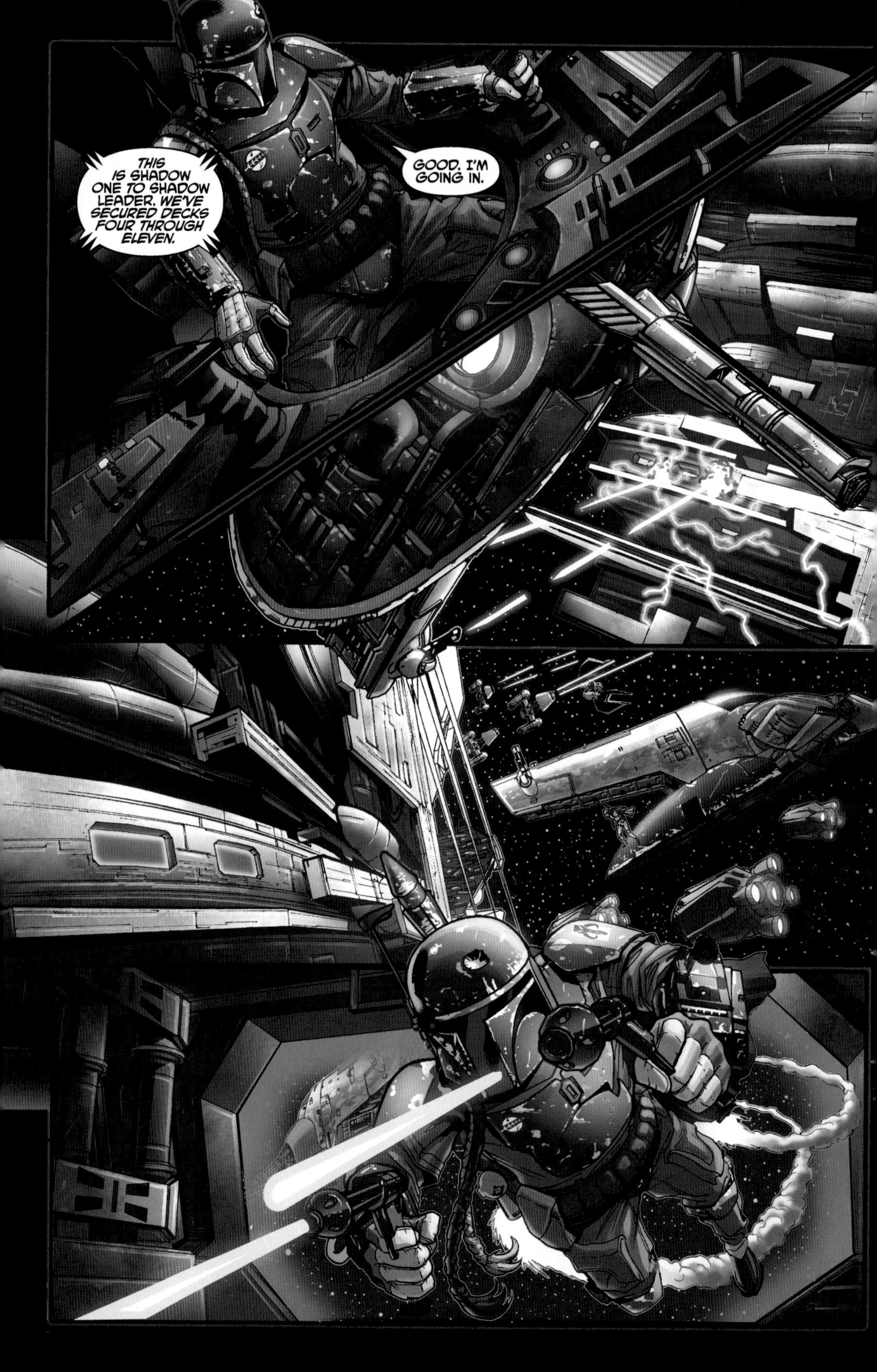
THIS IS SHADOW ONE TO SHADOW LEADER. WE'VE SECURED DECKS FOUR THROUGH ELEVEN.
GOOD. I'M GOING IN.

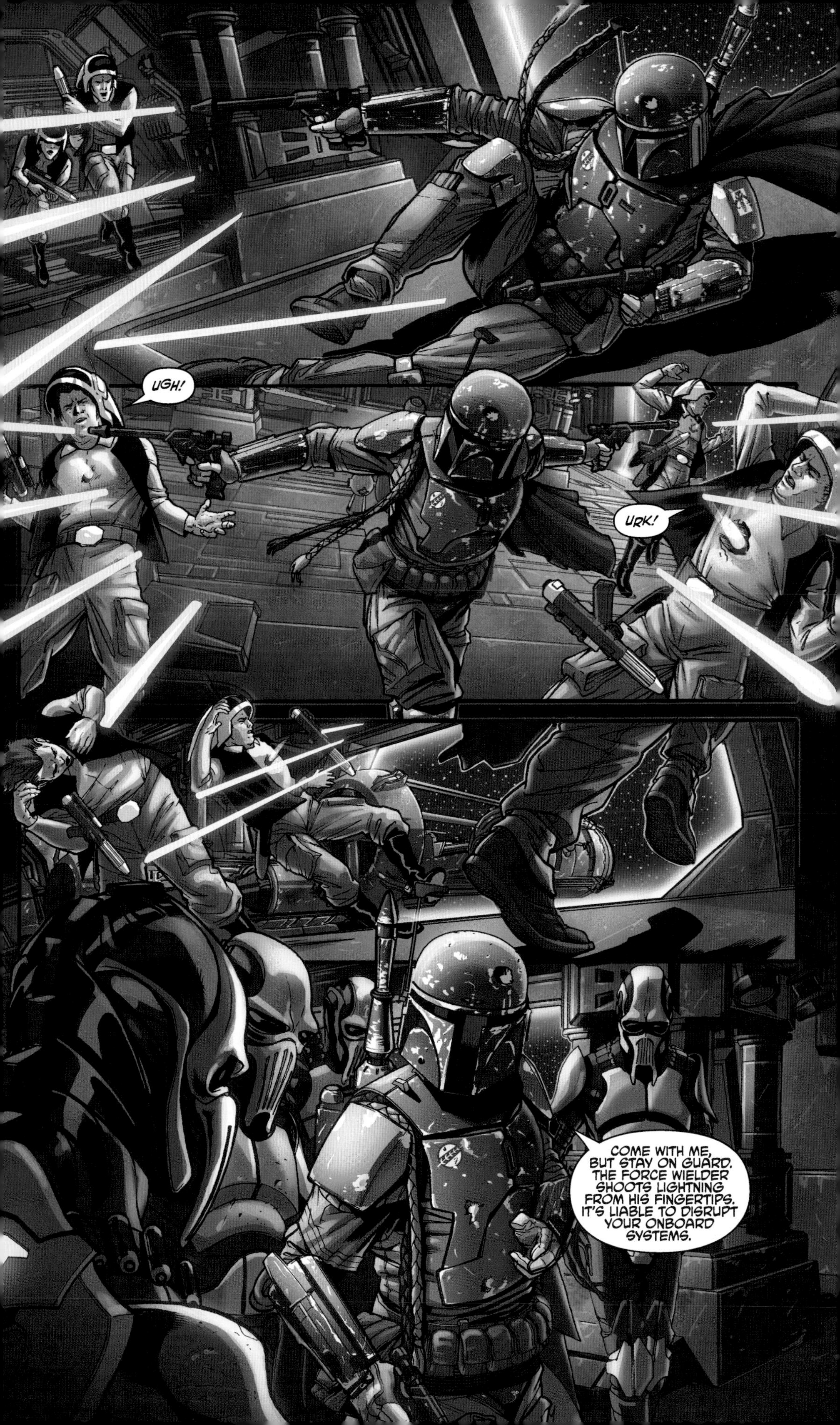
UGH!
URK!
COME WITH ME, BUT STAY ON GUARD. THE FORCE WIELDER SHOOTS LIGHTNING FROM HIS FINGERTIPS. IT'S LIABLE TO DISRUPT YOUR ONBOARD SYSTEMS.

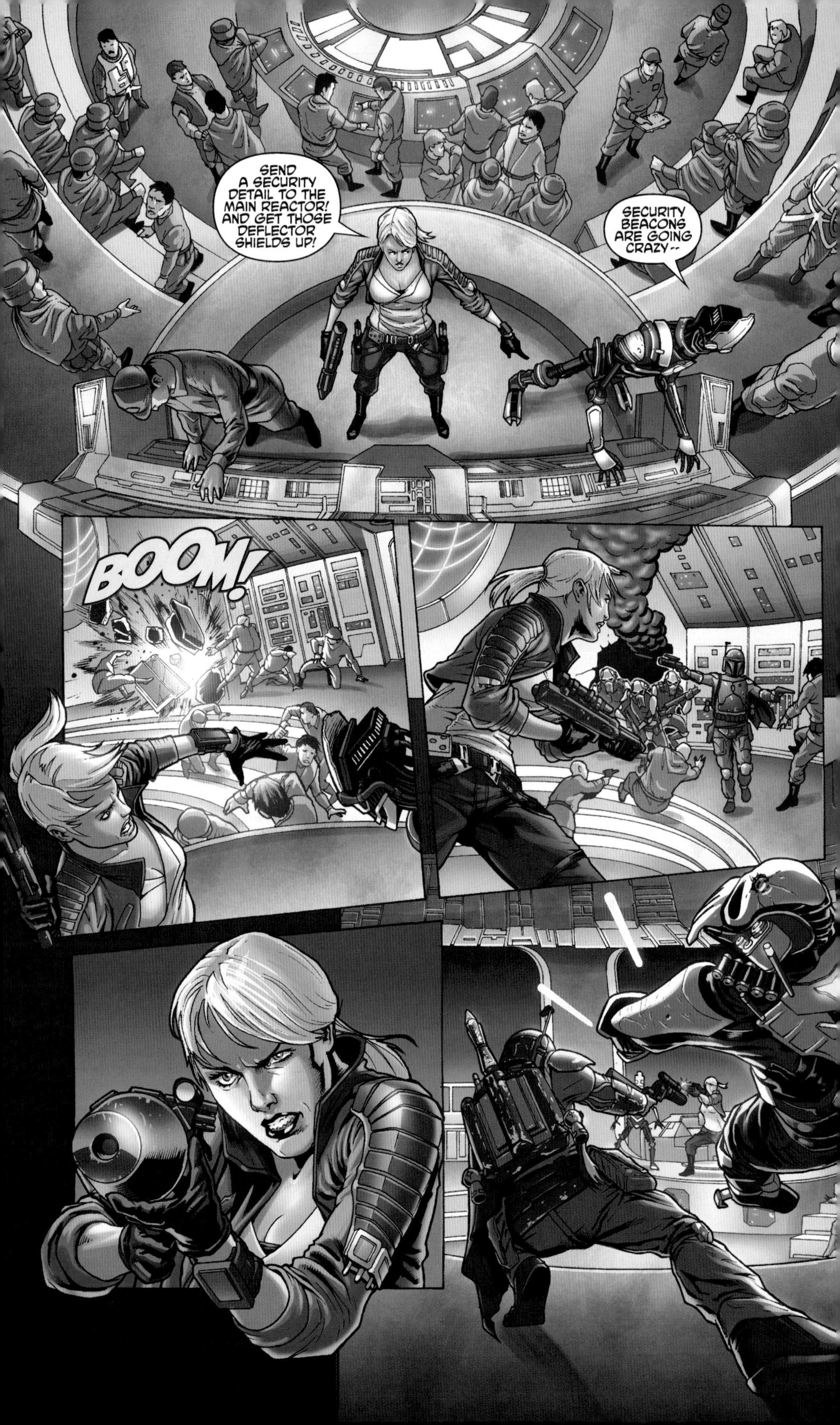
SEND A SECURITY DETAIL TO THE MAIN REACTOR! AND GET THOSE DEFLECTOR SHIELDS UP!
SECURITY BEACONS ARE GOING CRAZY--
BOOM!

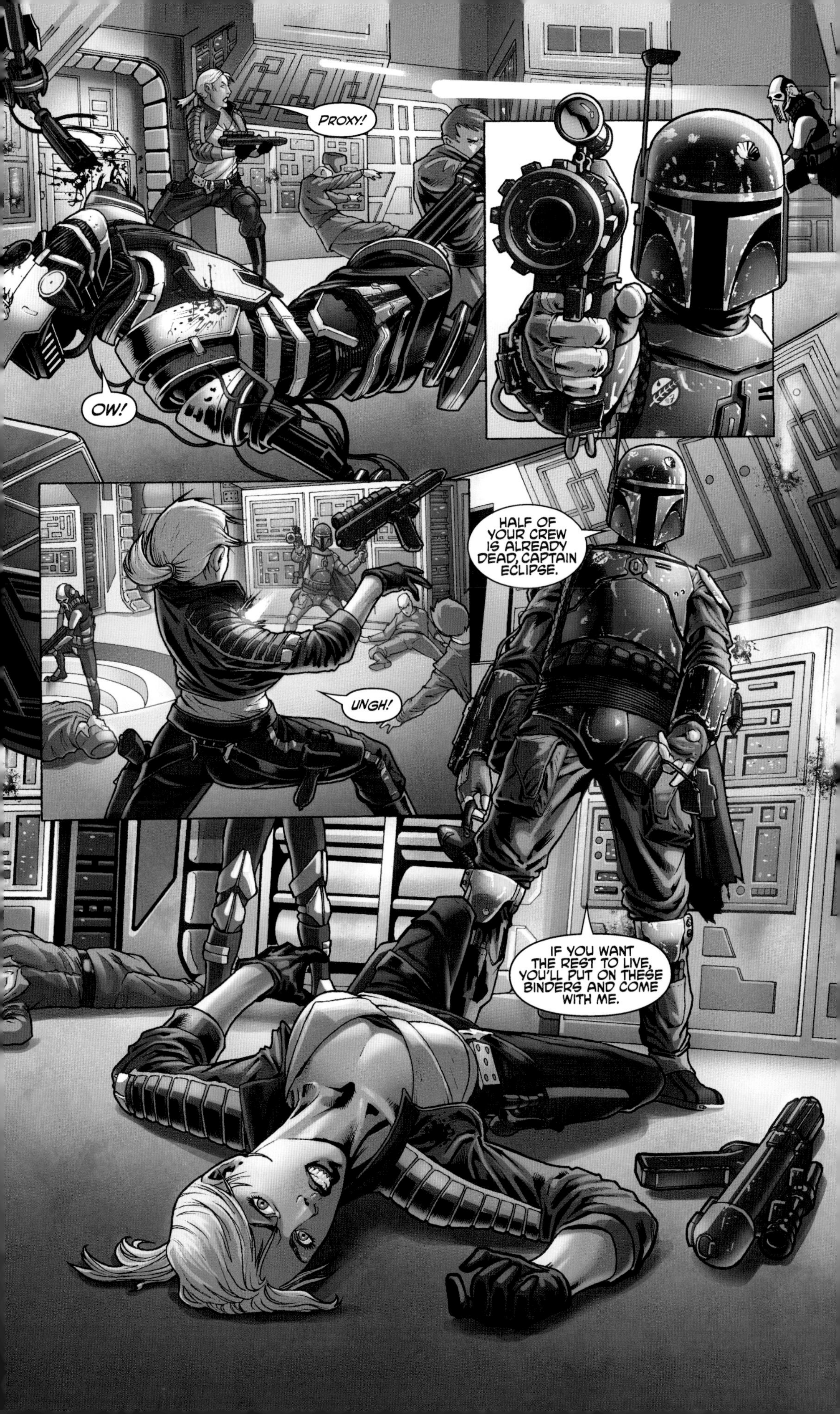
PROXY!
OW!
HALF OF YOUR CREW IS ALREADY DEAD, CAPTAIN ECLIPSE.
UNGH!
IF YOU WANT THE REST TO LIVE, YOU'LL PUT ON THESE BINDERS AND COME WITH ME.

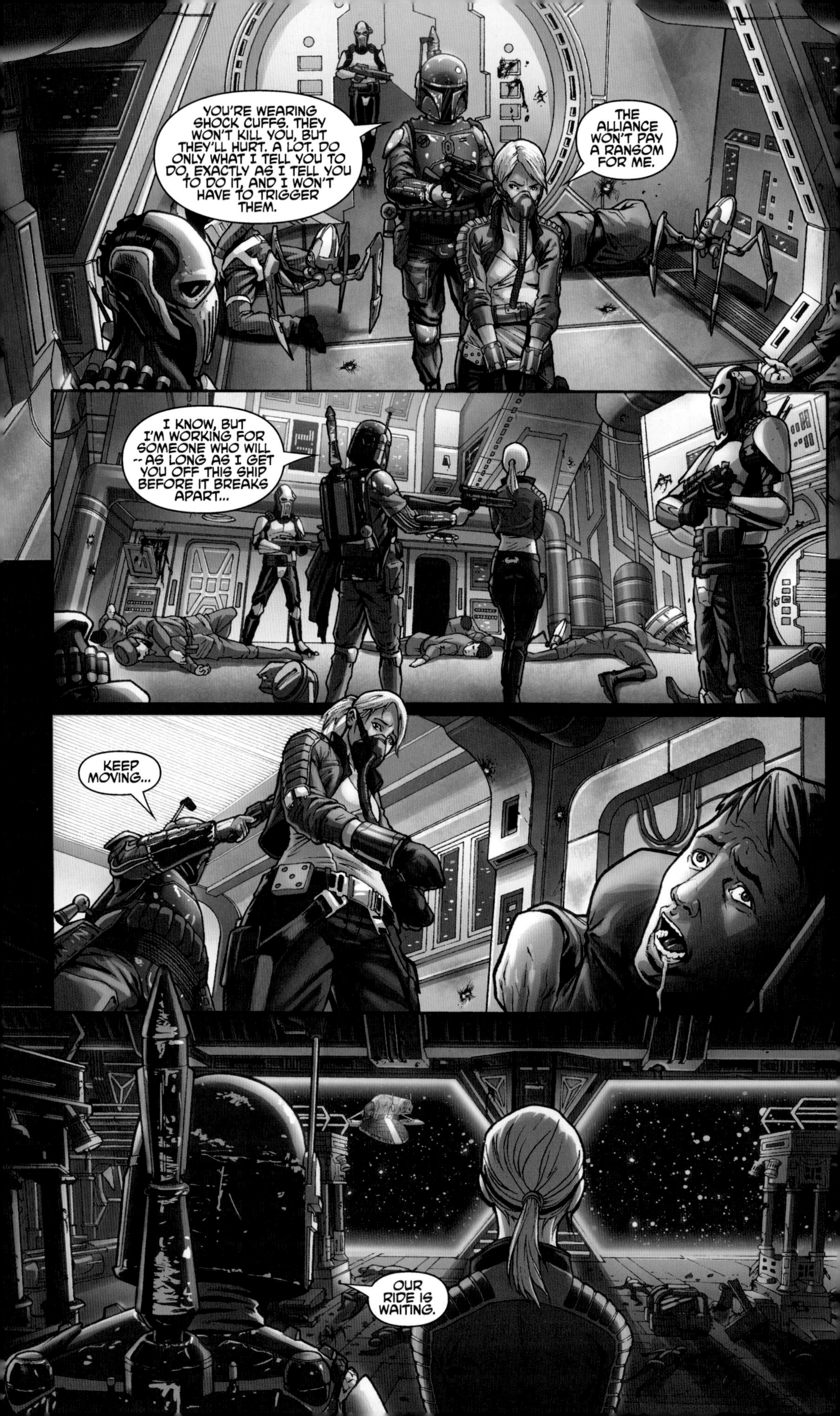
YOU'RE WEARING SHOCK CUFFS. THEY WON'T KILL YOU, BUT THEY'LL HURT. A LOT. DO ONLY WHAT I TELL YOU TO DO, EXACTLY AS I TELL YOU TO DO IT, AND I WON'T HAVE TO TRIGGER THEM.
THE ALLIANCE WON'T PAY A RANSOM FOR ME.
I KNOW, BUT I'M WORKING FOR SOMEONE WHO WILL --AS LONG AS I GET YOU OFF THIS SHIP BEFORE IT BREAKS APART...
KEEP MOVING...
OUR RIDE IS WAITING.

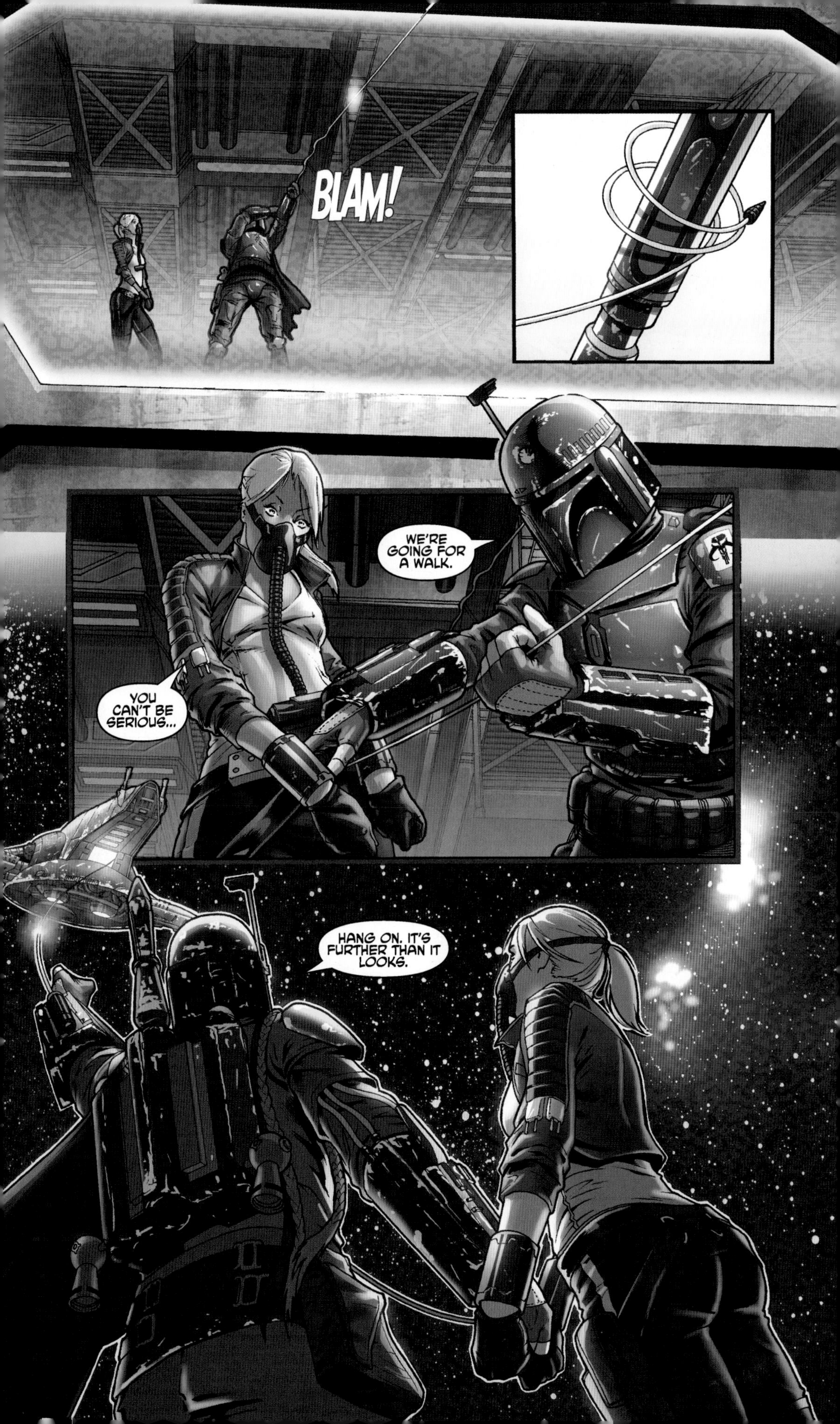
BLAM!
WE'RE GOING FOR A WALK.
YOU CAN'T BE SERIOUS...
HANG ON. IT'S FURTHER THAN IT LOOKS.

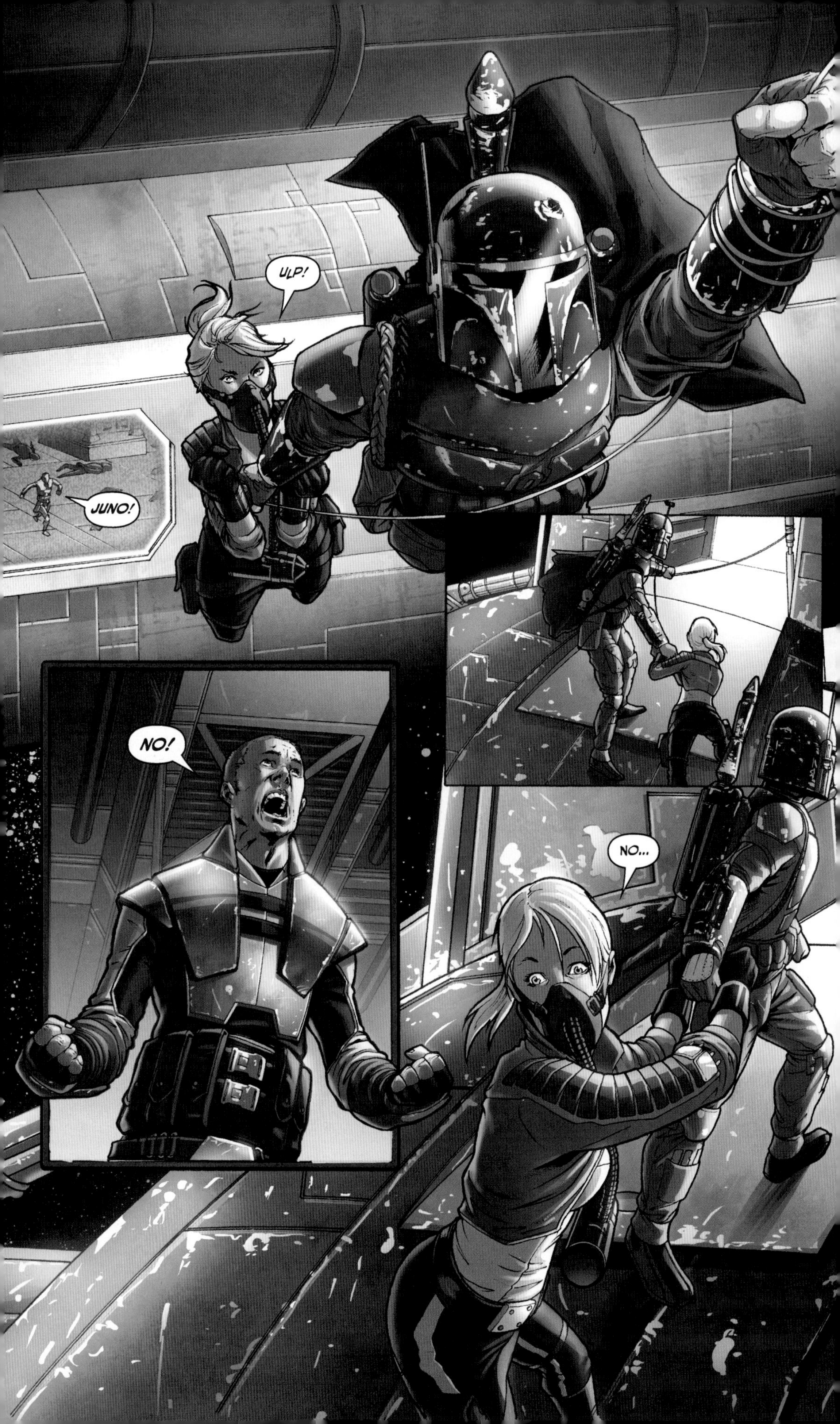
ULP!
JUNO!
NO!
NO...

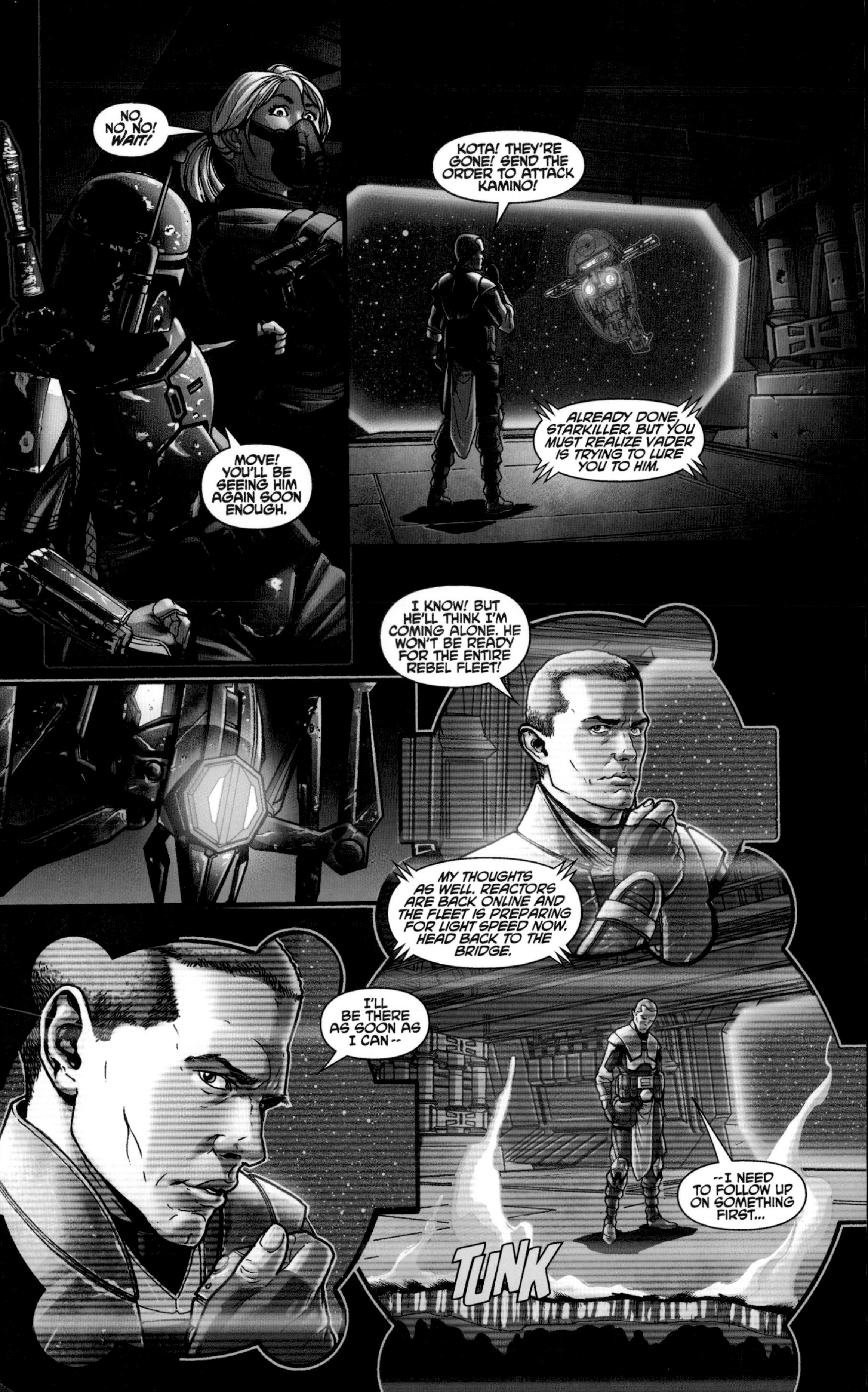
NO, NO, NO! WAIT!
MOVE! YOU'LL BE SEEING HIM AGAIN SOON ENOUGH.
KOTA! THEY'RE GONE! SEND THE ORDER TO ATTACK KAMINO!
ALREADY DONE, STARKILLER. BUT YOU MUST REALIZE VADER IS TRYING TO LURE YOU TO HIM.
I KNOW! BUT HE'LL THINK I'M COMING ALONE. HE WON'T BE READY FOR THE ENTIRE REBEL FLEET!
MY THOUGHTS AS WELL. REACTORS ARE BACK ONLINE AND THE FLEET IS PREPARING FOR LIGHT SPEED NOW. HEAD BACK TO THE BRIDGE.
I'LL BE THERE AS SOON AS I CAN--
--I NEED TO FOLLOW UP ON SOMETHING FIRST...
TUNK

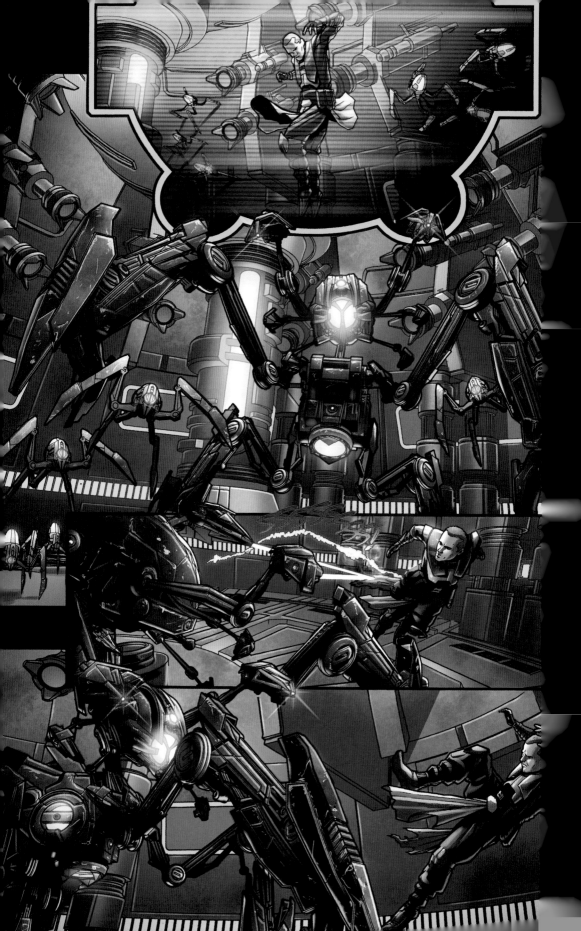

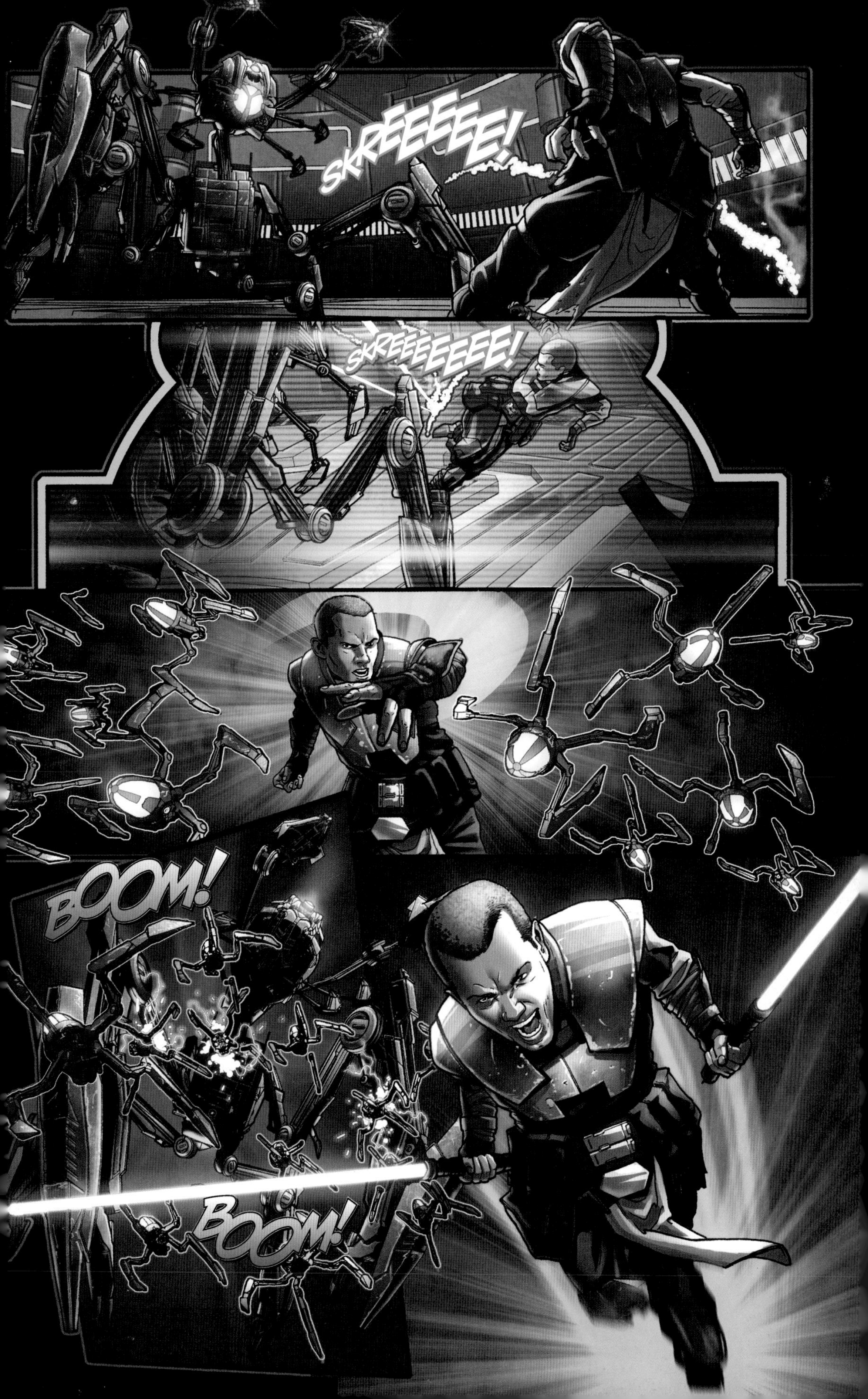
SKREEEEEEE!
SKREEEEEEEE!
BOOM!
BOOM!

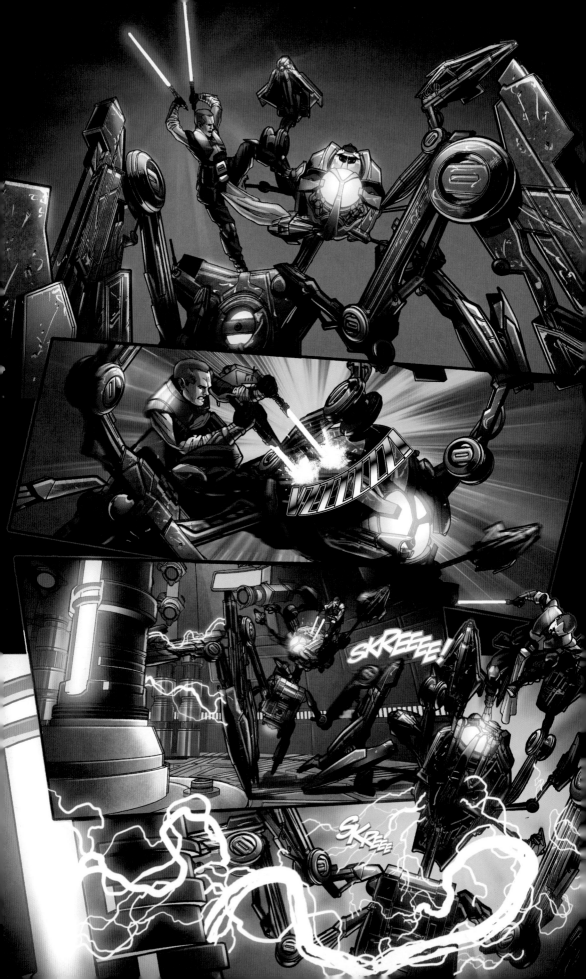

SKREEEEE!

VZZZZZZ

SKREEEE

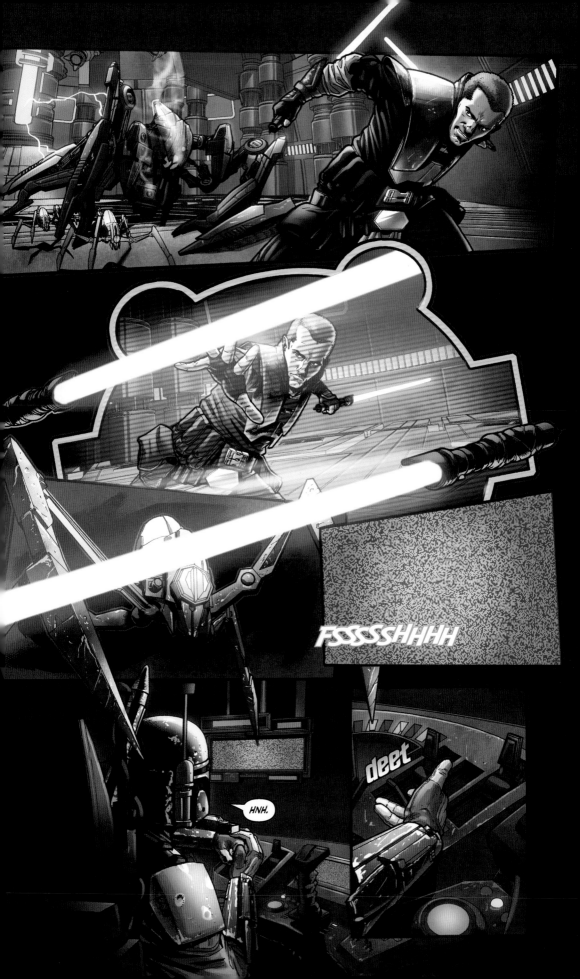

FSSSSSHHHH

deet

HNH.

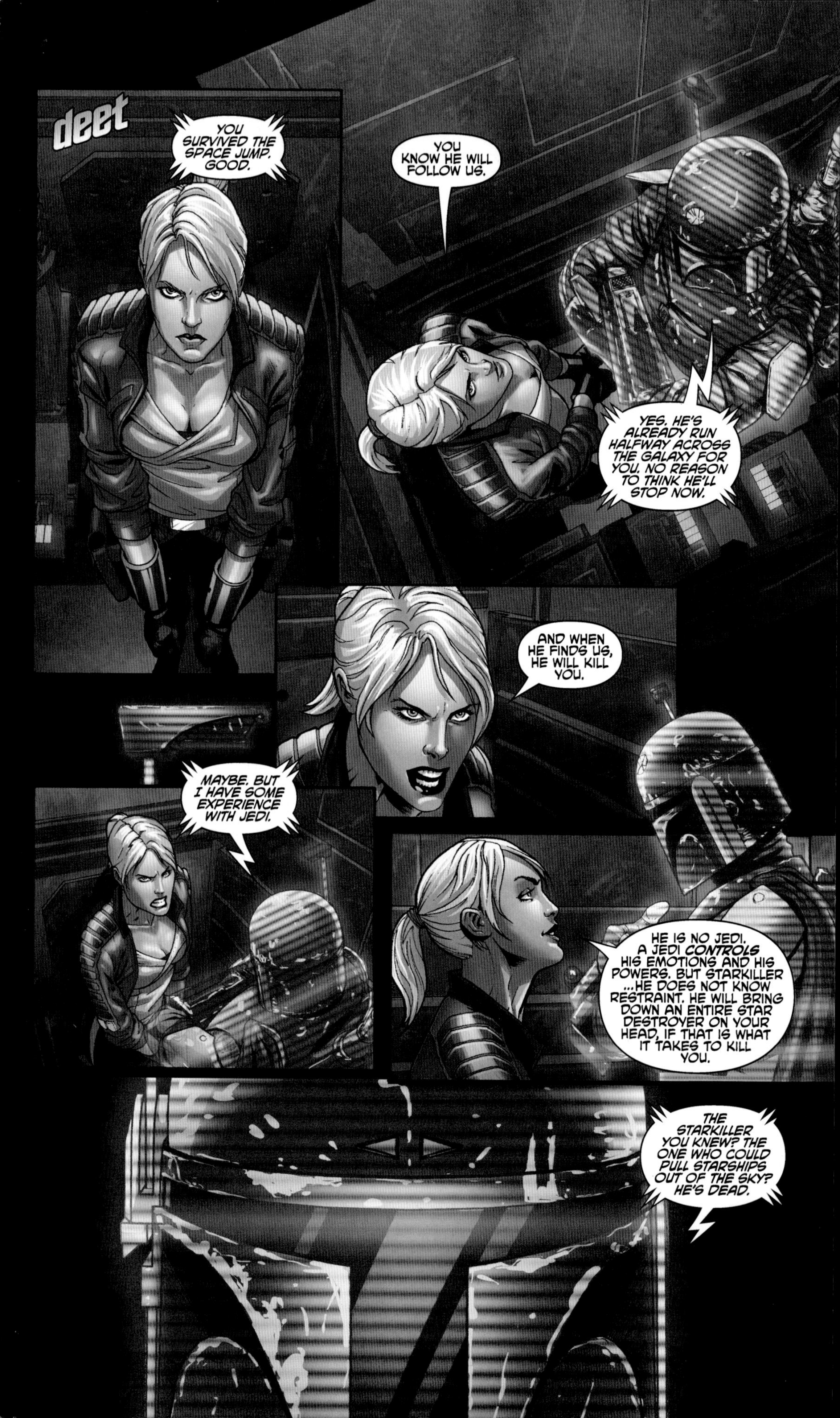
deet
YOU SURVIVED THE SPACE JUMP. GOOD.
YOU KNOW HE WILL FOLLOW US.
YES. HE'S ALREADY RUN HALFWAY ACROSS THE GALAXY FOR YOU. NO REASON TO THINK HE'LL STOP NOW.
AND WHEN HE FINDS US, HE WILL KILL YOU.
MAYBE. BUT I HAVE SOME EXPERIENCE WITH JEDI.
HE IS NO JEDI. A JEDI *CONTROLS* HIS EMOTIONS AND HIS POWERS. BUT STARKILLER ...HE DOES NOT KNOW RESTRAINT. HE WILL BRING DOWN AN ENTIRE STAR DESTROYER ON YOUR HEAD, IF THAT IS WHAT IT TAKES TO KILL YOU.
THE STARKILLER YOU KNEW? THE ONE WHO COULD PULL STARSHIPS OUT OF THE SKY? HE'S DEAD.

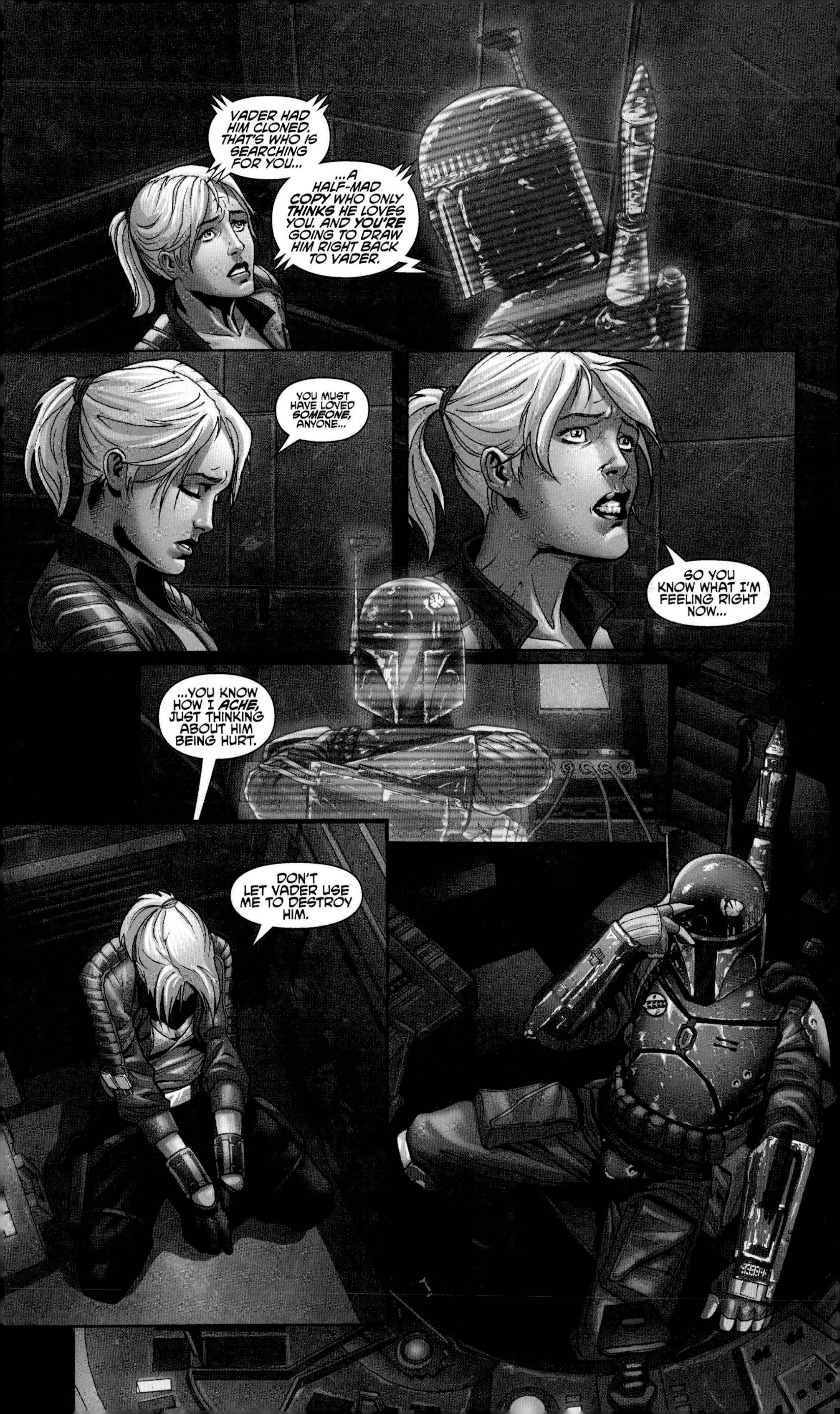
VADER HAD HIM CLONED. THAT'S WHO IS SEARCHING FOR YOU...
...A HALF-MAD COPY WHO ONLY THINKS HE LOVES YOU. AND YOU'RE GOING TO DRAW HIM RIGHT BACK TO VADER.
YOU MUST HAVE LOVED SOMEONE, ANYONE...
SO YOU KNOW WHAT I'M FEELING RIGHT NOW...
...YOU KNOW HOW I ACHE, JUST THINKING ABOUT HIM BEING HURT.
DON'T LET VADER USE ME TO DESTROY HIM.

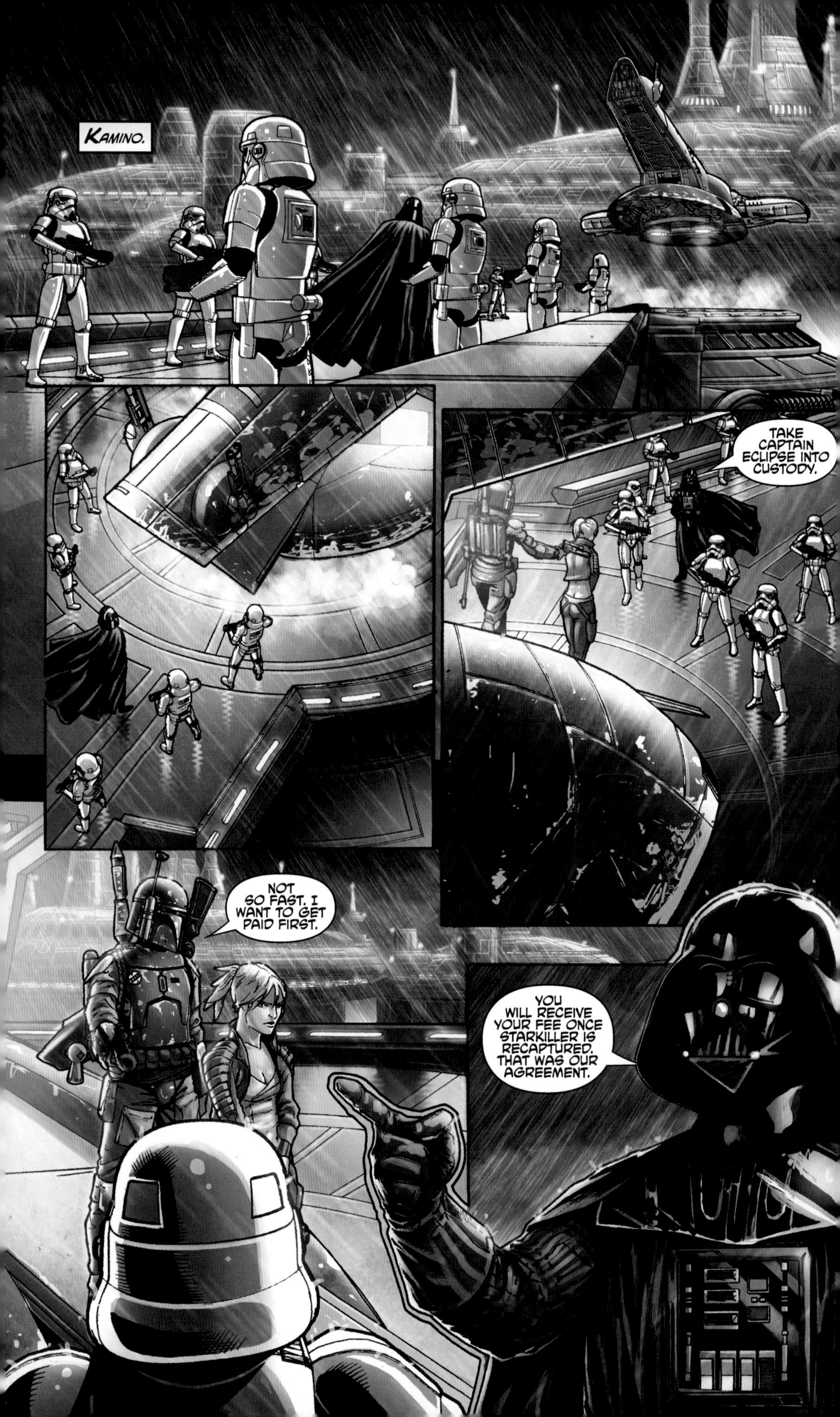
KAMINO.
TAKE CAPTAIN ECLIPSE INTO CUSTODY.
NOT SO FAST. I WANT TO GET PAID FIRST.
YOU WILL RECEIVE YOUR FEE ONCE STARKILLER IS RECAPTURED. THAT WAS OUR AGREEMENT.

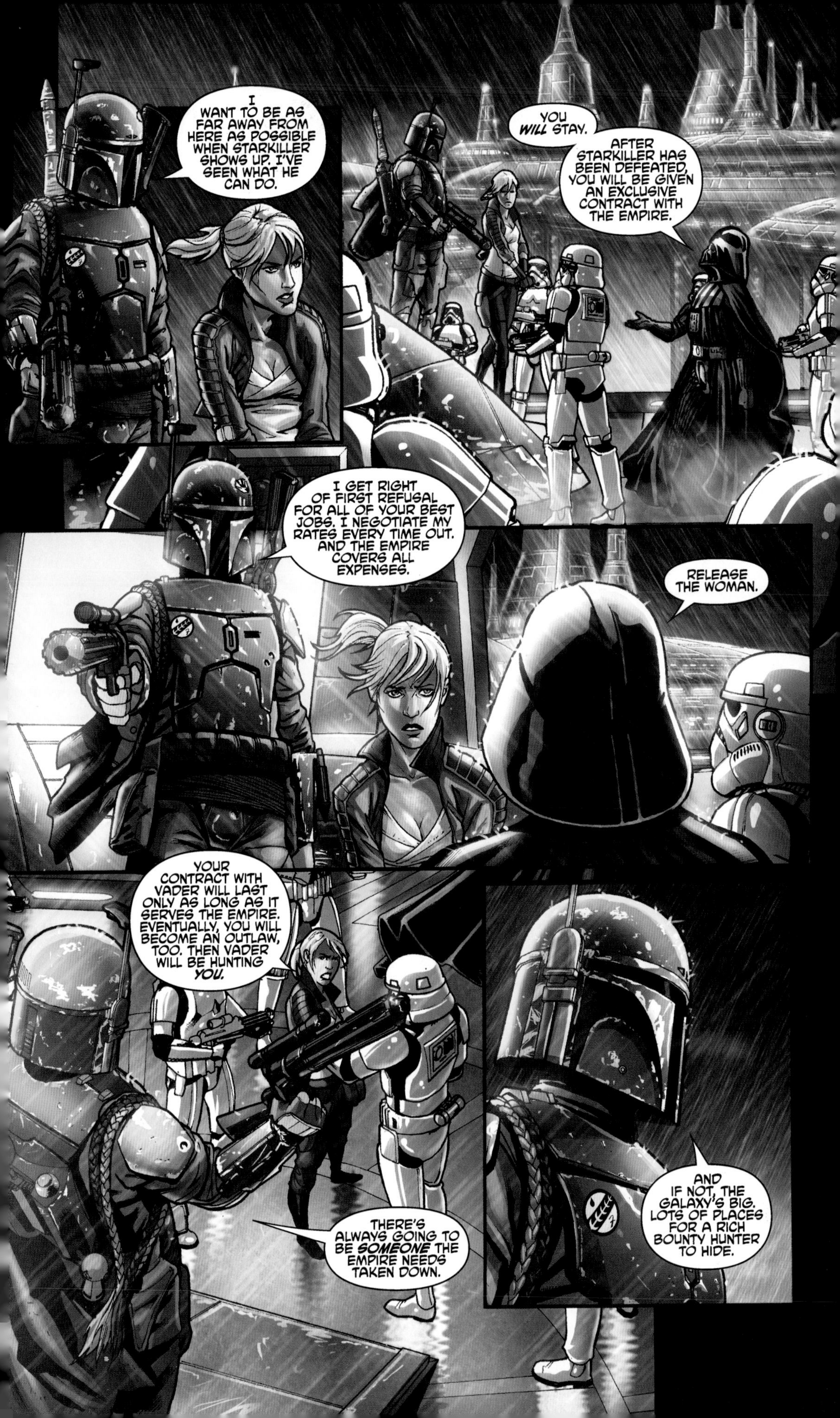
I WANT TO BE AS FAR AWAY FROM HERE AS POSSIBLE WHEN STARKILLER SHOWS UP. I'VE SEEN WHAT HE CAN DO.
YOU *WILL* STAY.
AFTER STARKILLER HAS BEEN DEFEATED, YOU WILL BE GIVEN AN EXCLUSIVE CONTRACT WITH THE EMPIRE.
I GET RIGHT OF FIRST REFUSAL FOR ALL OF YOUR BEST JOBS. I NEGOTIATE MY RATES EVERY TIME OUT. AND THE EMPIRE COVERS ALL EXPENSES.
RELEASE THE WOMAN.
YOUR CONTRACT WITH VADER WILL LAST ONLY AS LONG AS IT SERVES THE EMPIRE. EVENTUALLY, YOU WILL BECOME AN OUTLAW, TOO. THEN VADER WILL BE HUNTING *YOU.*
THERE'S ALWAYS GOING TO BE *SOMEONE* THE EMPIRE NEEDS TAKEN DOWN.
AND IF NOT, THE GALAXY'S BIG. LOTS OF PLACES FOR A RICH BOUNTY HUNTER TO HIDE.

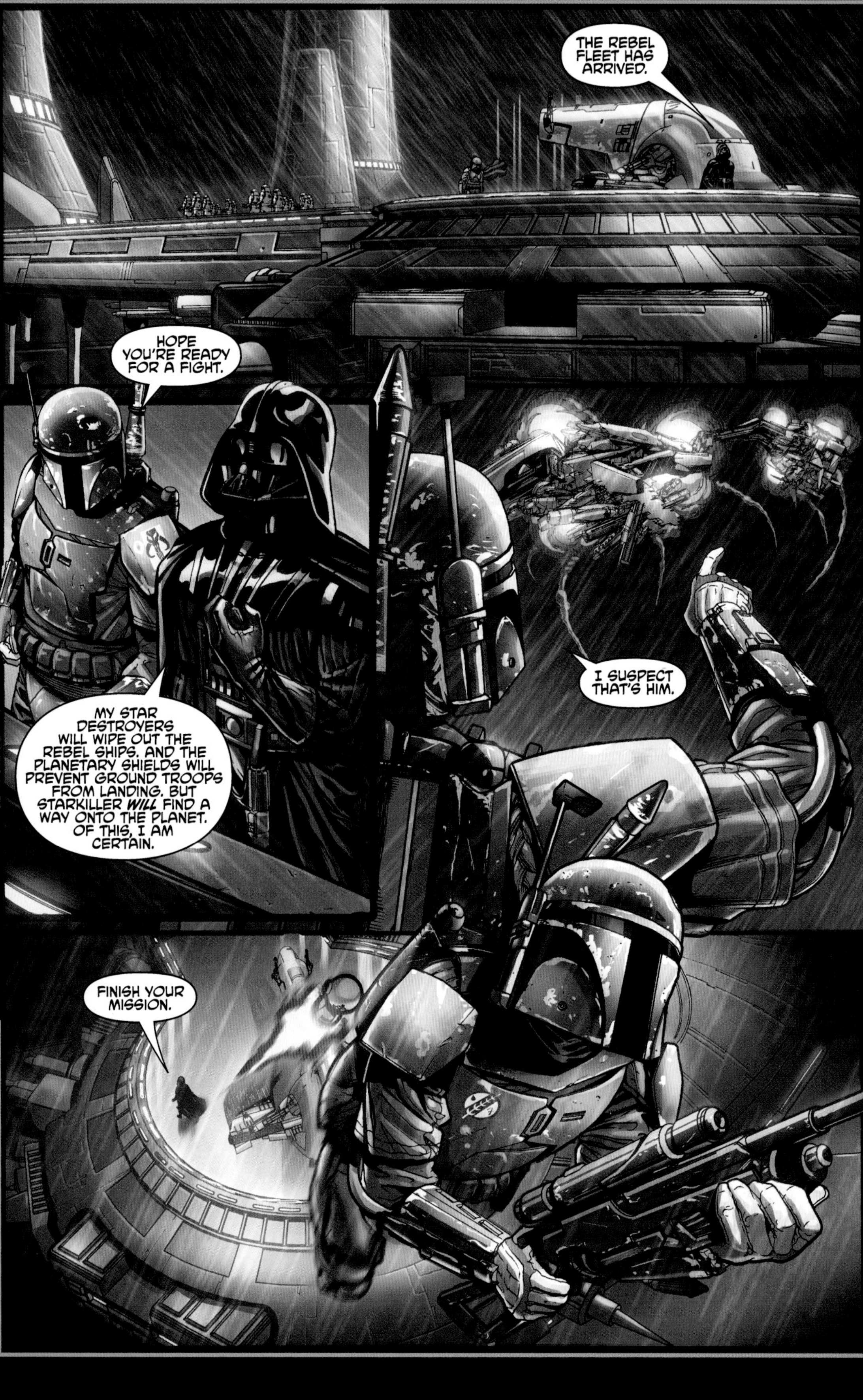
THE REBEL FLEET HAS ARRIVED.
HOPE YOU'RE READY FOR A FIGHT.
MY STAR DESTROYERS WILL WIPE OUT THE REBEL SHIPS. AND THE PLANETARY SHIELDS WILL PREVENT GROUND TROOPS FROM LANDING. BUT STARKILLER WILL FIND A WAY ONTO THE PLANET. OF THIS, I AM CERTAIN.
I SUSPECT THAT'S HIM.
FINISH YOUR MISSION.

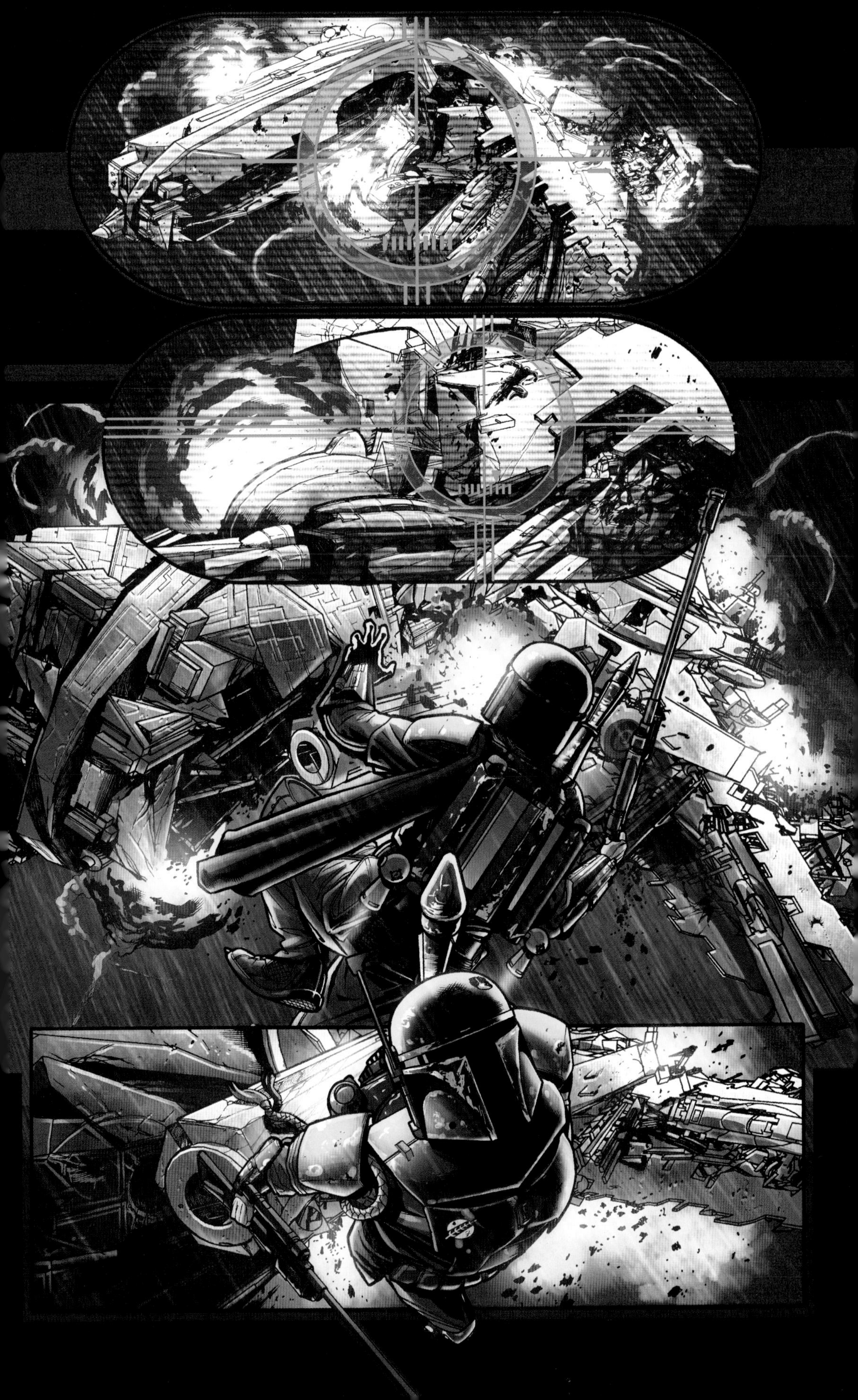

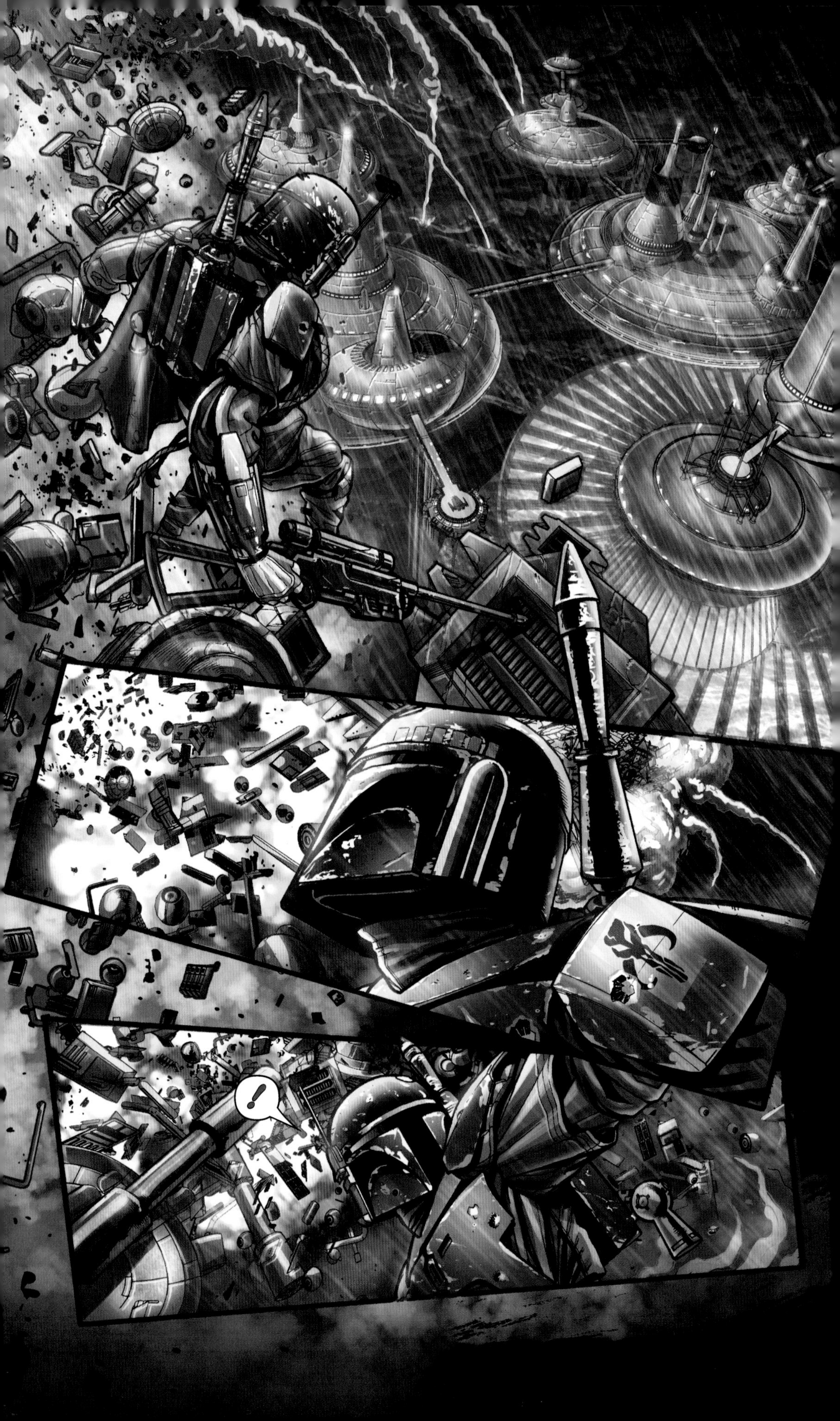
!

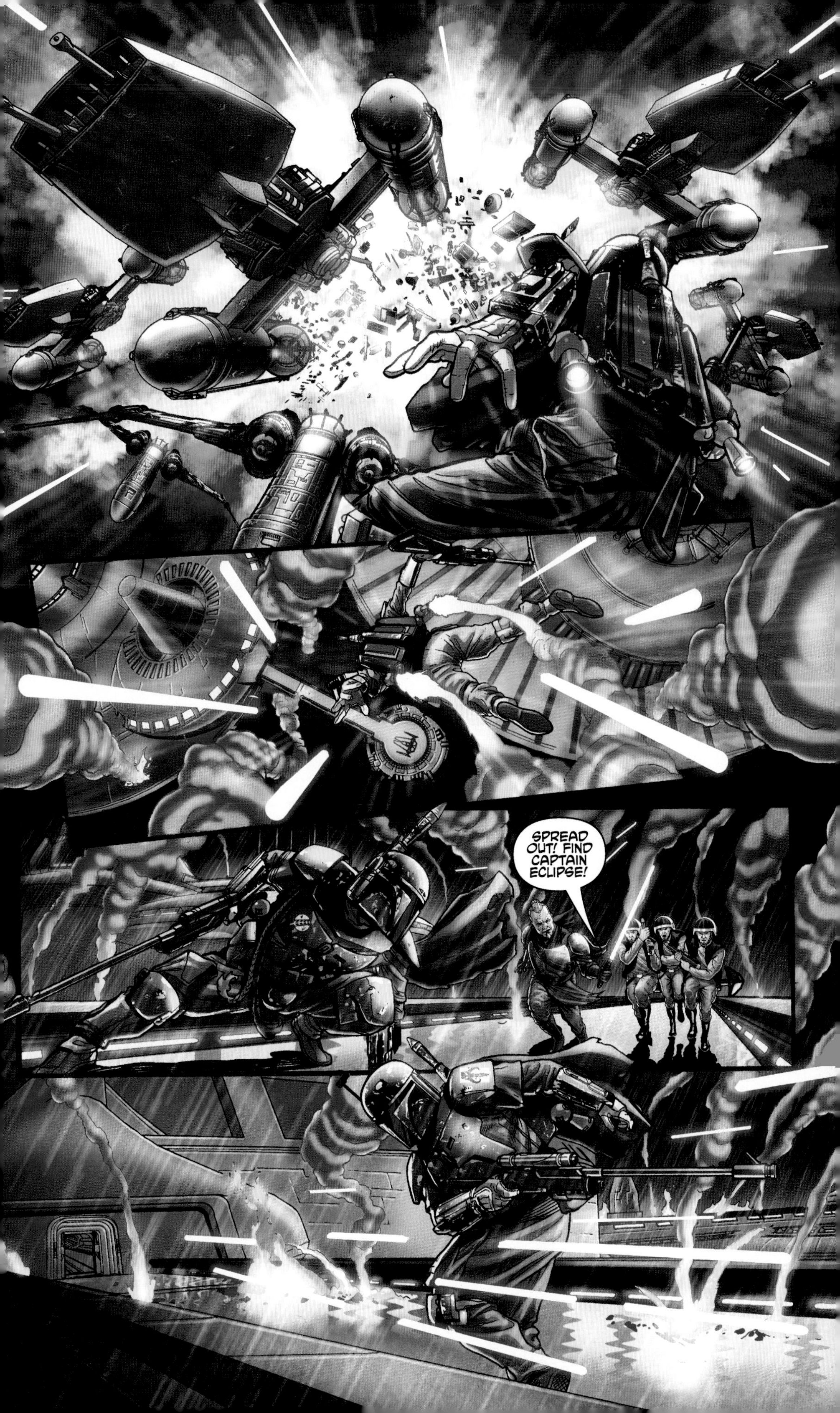
SPREAD OUT! FIND CAPTAIN ECLIPSE!

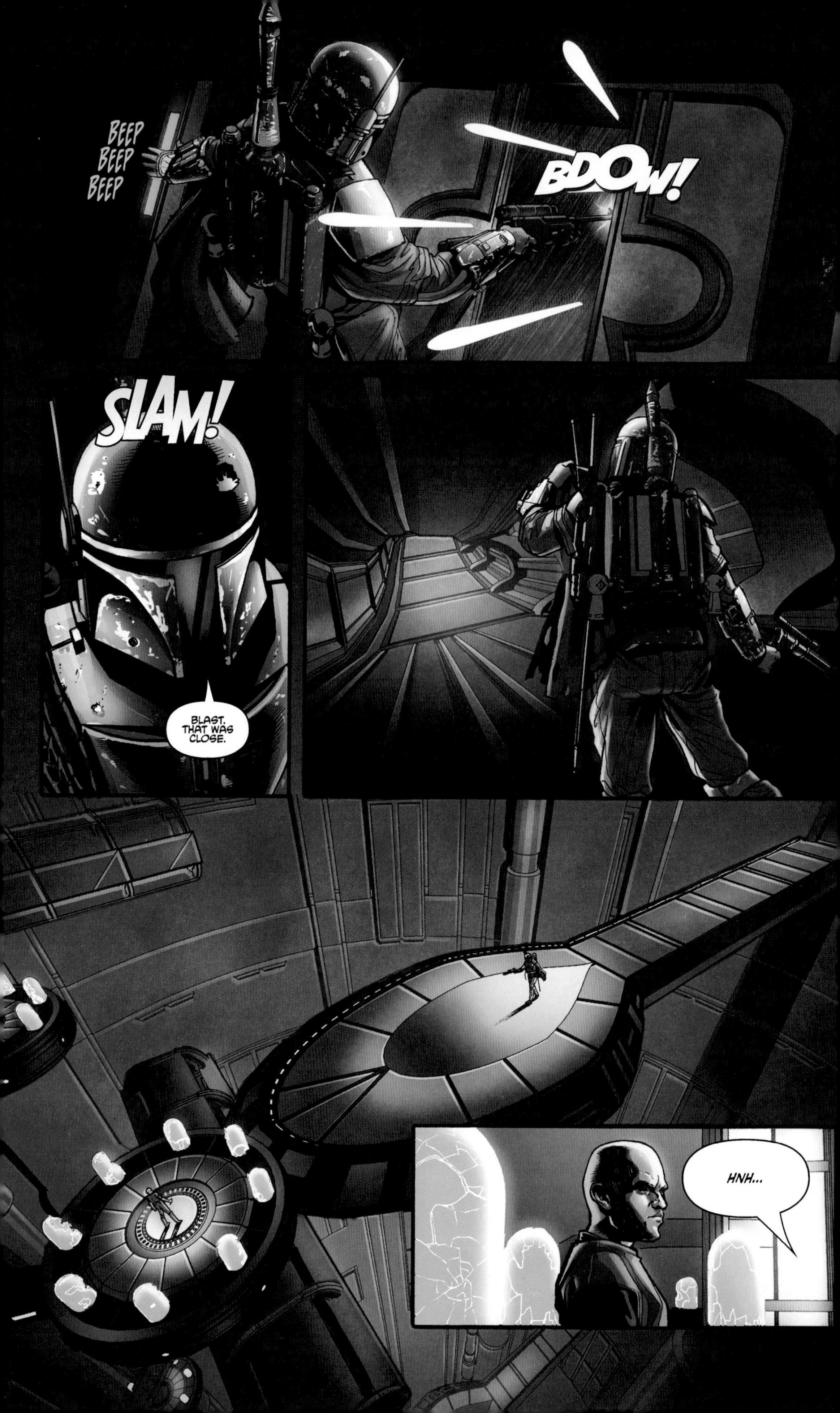
BEEP BEEP BEEP
BDOW!
SLAM!
BLAST. THAT WAS CLOSE.
HNH...

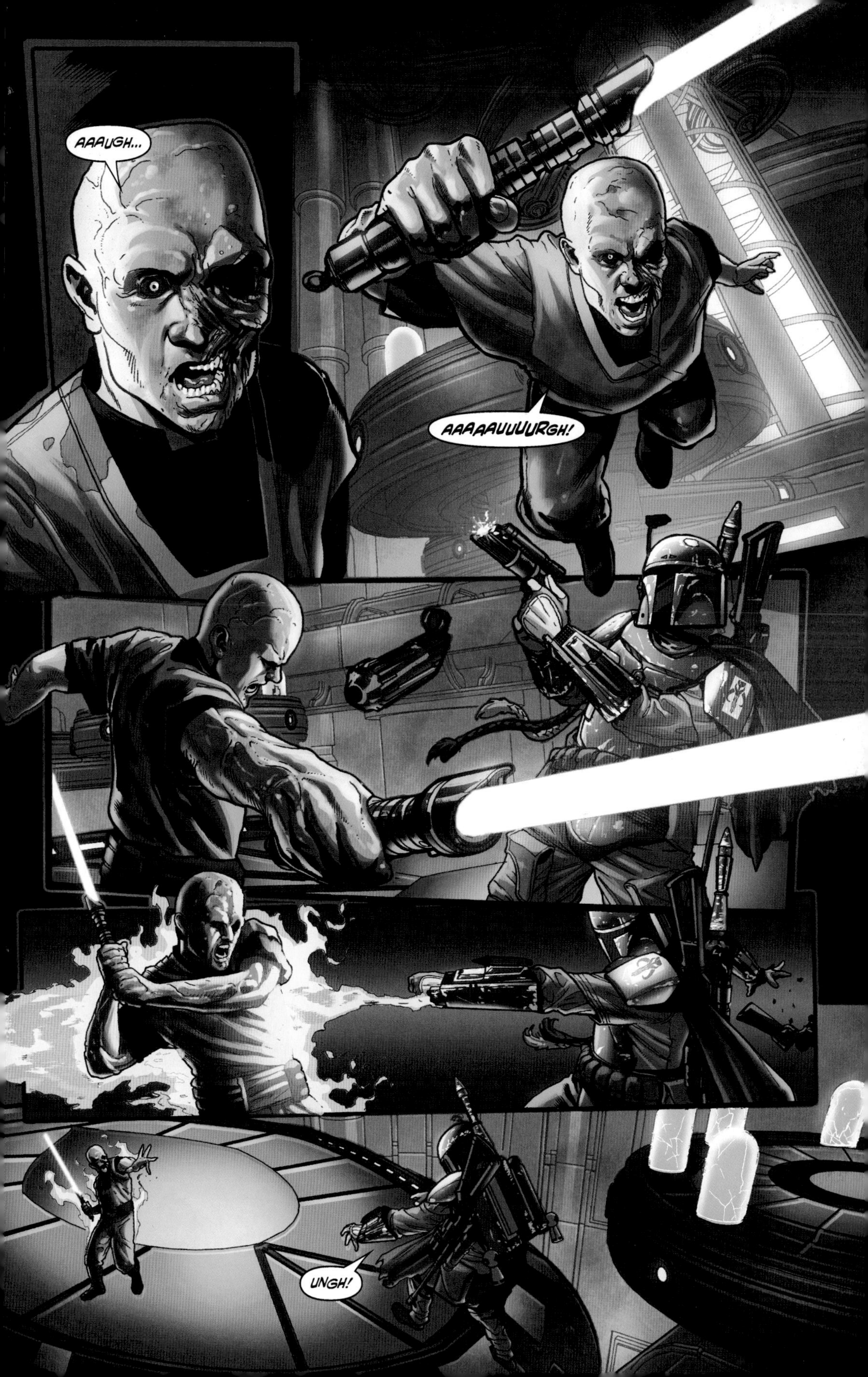
AAAUGH...
AAAAAUUUURGH!
UNGH!

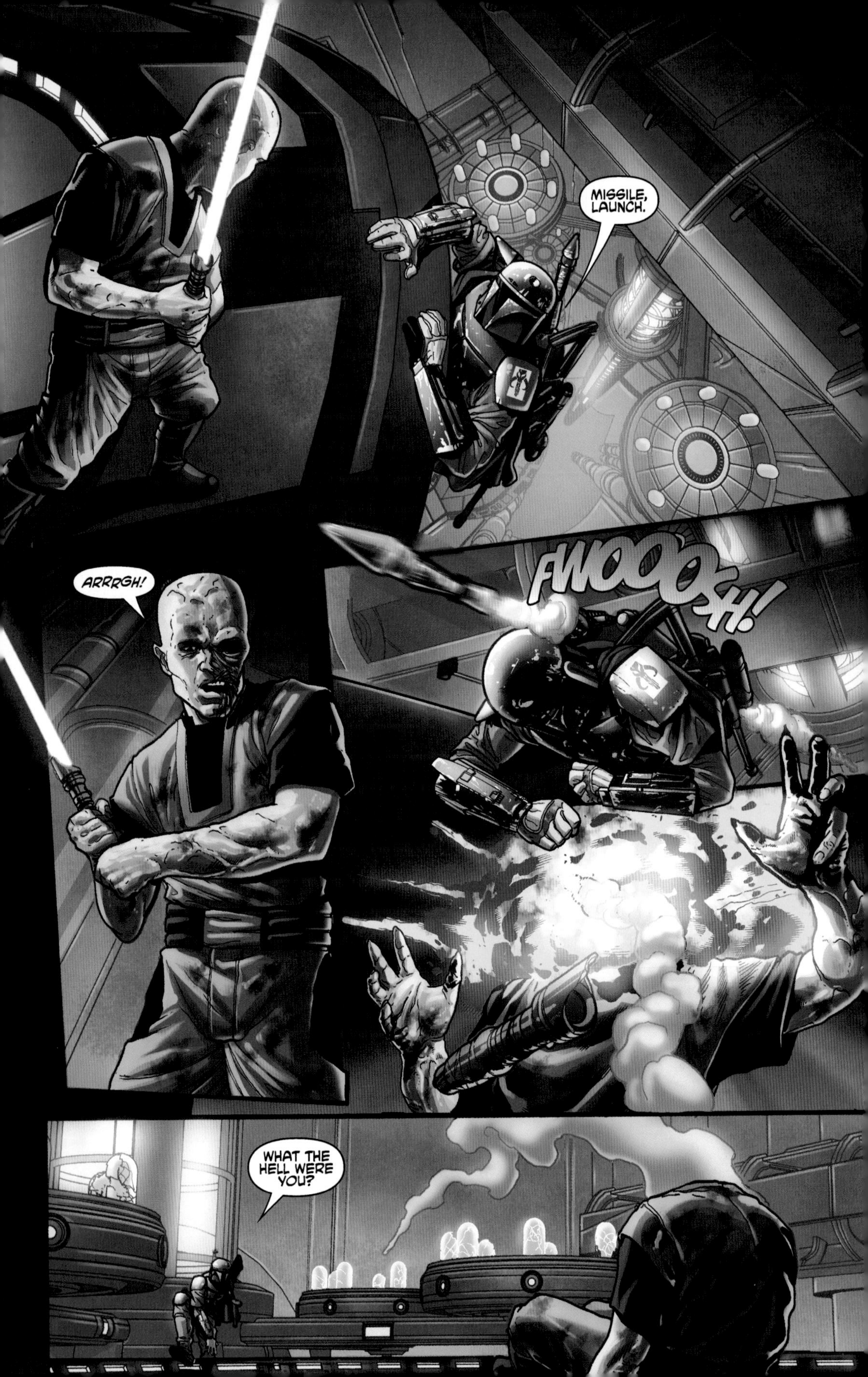
MISSILE, LAUNCH.
ARRRGH!
FWOOOSH!
WHAT THE HELL WERE YOU?

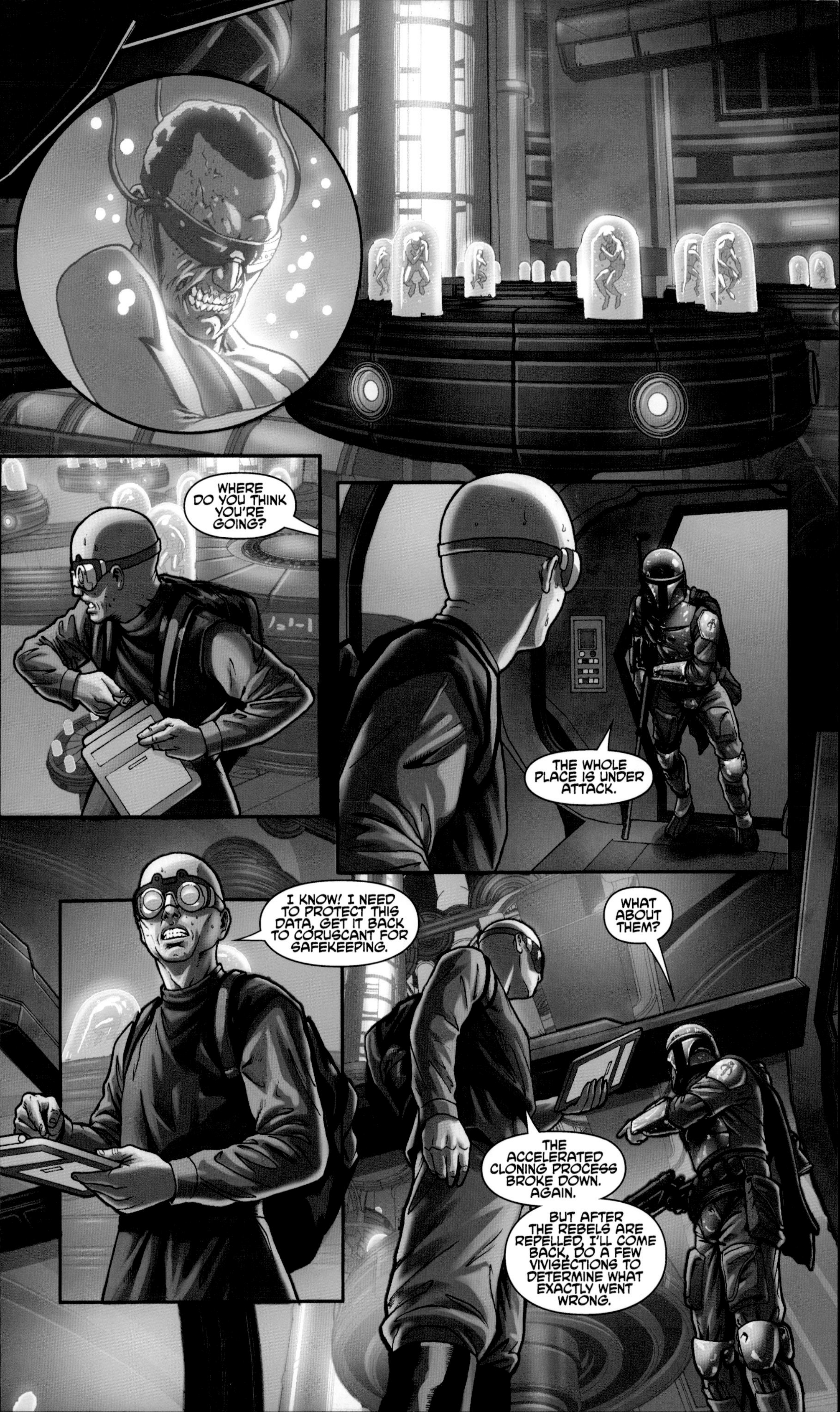
WHERE DO YOU THINK YOU'RE GOING?
THE WHOLE PLACE IS UNDER ATTACK.
I KNOW! I NEED TO PROTECT THIS DATA, GET IT BACK TO CORUSCANT FOR SAFEKEEPING.
WHAT ABOUT THEM?
THE ACCELERATED CLONING PROCESS BROKE DOWN. AGAIN.
BUT AFTER THE REBELS ARE REPELLED, I'LL COME BACK, DO A FEW VIVISECTIONS TO DETERMINE WHAT EXACTLY WENT WRONG.

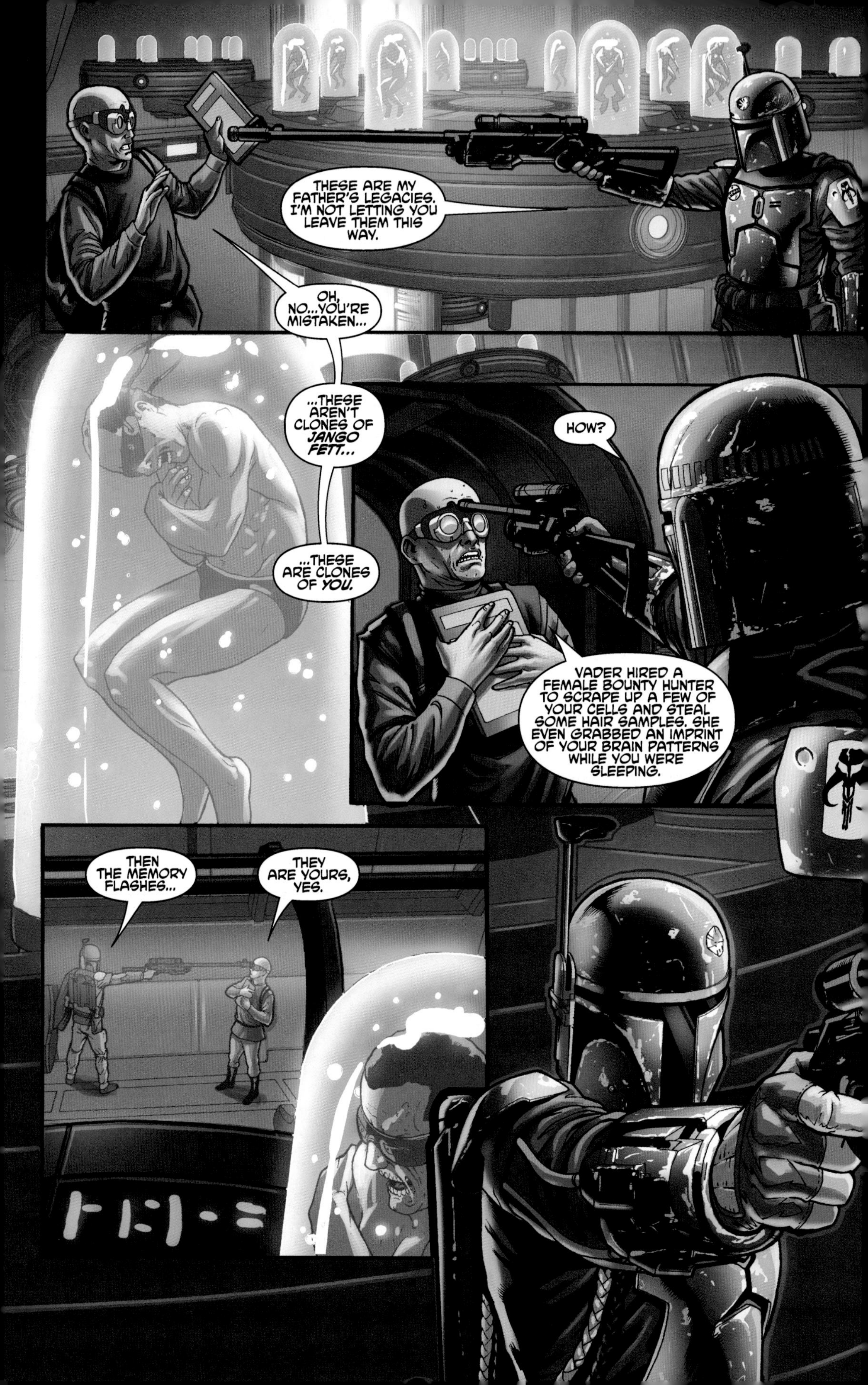
THESE ARE MY FATHER'S LEGACIES. I'M NOT LETTING YOU LEAVE THEM THIS WAY.
OH, NO...YOU'RE MISTAKEN...
...THESE AREN'T CLONES OF JANGO FETT...
...THESE ARE CLONES OF YOU.
HOW?
VADER HIRED A FEMALE BOUNTY HUNTER TO SCRAPE UP A FEW OF YOUR CELLS AND STEAL SOME HAIR SAMPLES. SHE EVEN GRABBED AN IMPRINT OF YOUR BRAIN PATTERNS WHILE YOU WERE SLEEPING.
THEN THE MEMORY FLASHES...
THEY ARE YOURS, YES.

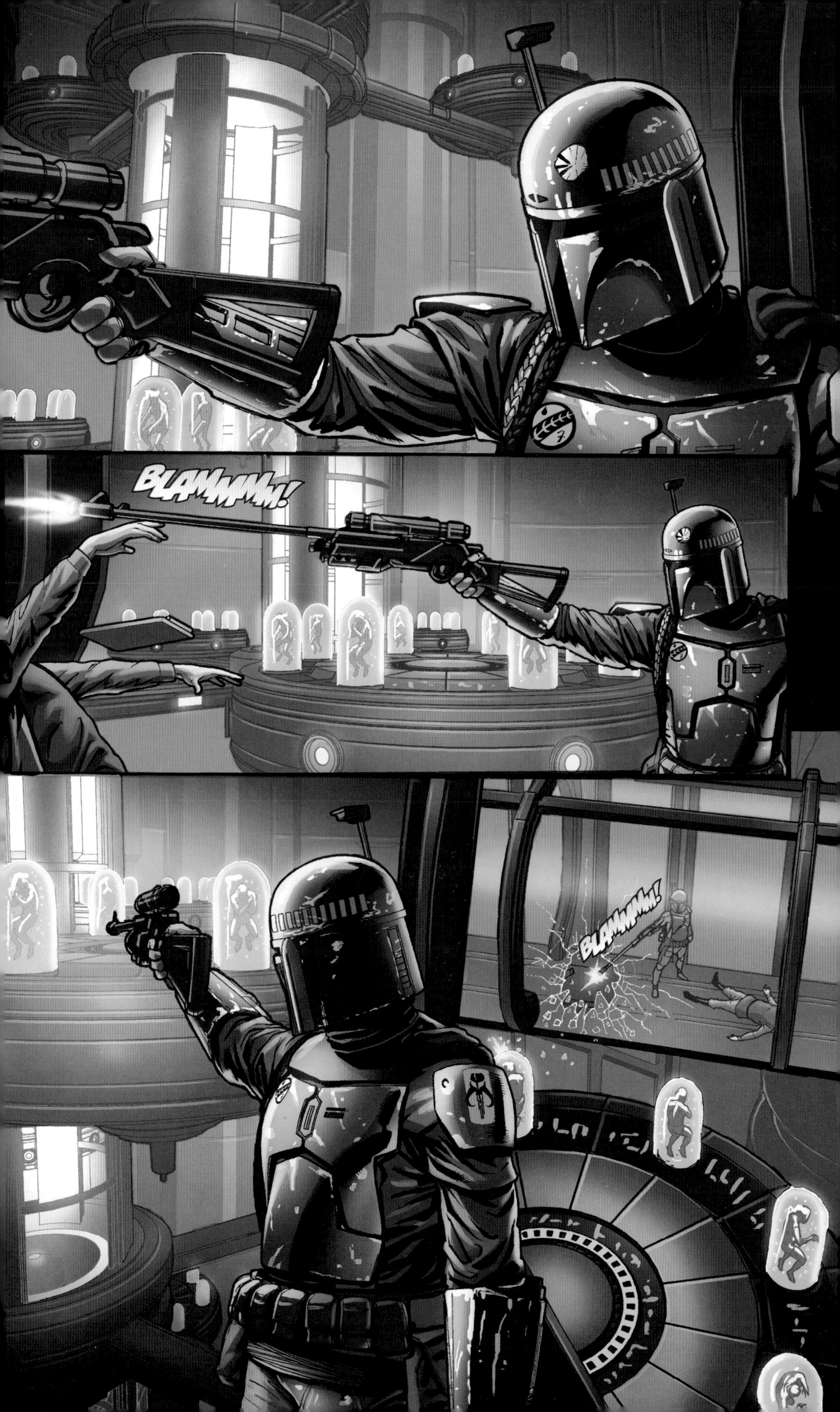
BLAMMMM!
BLAMMMM!

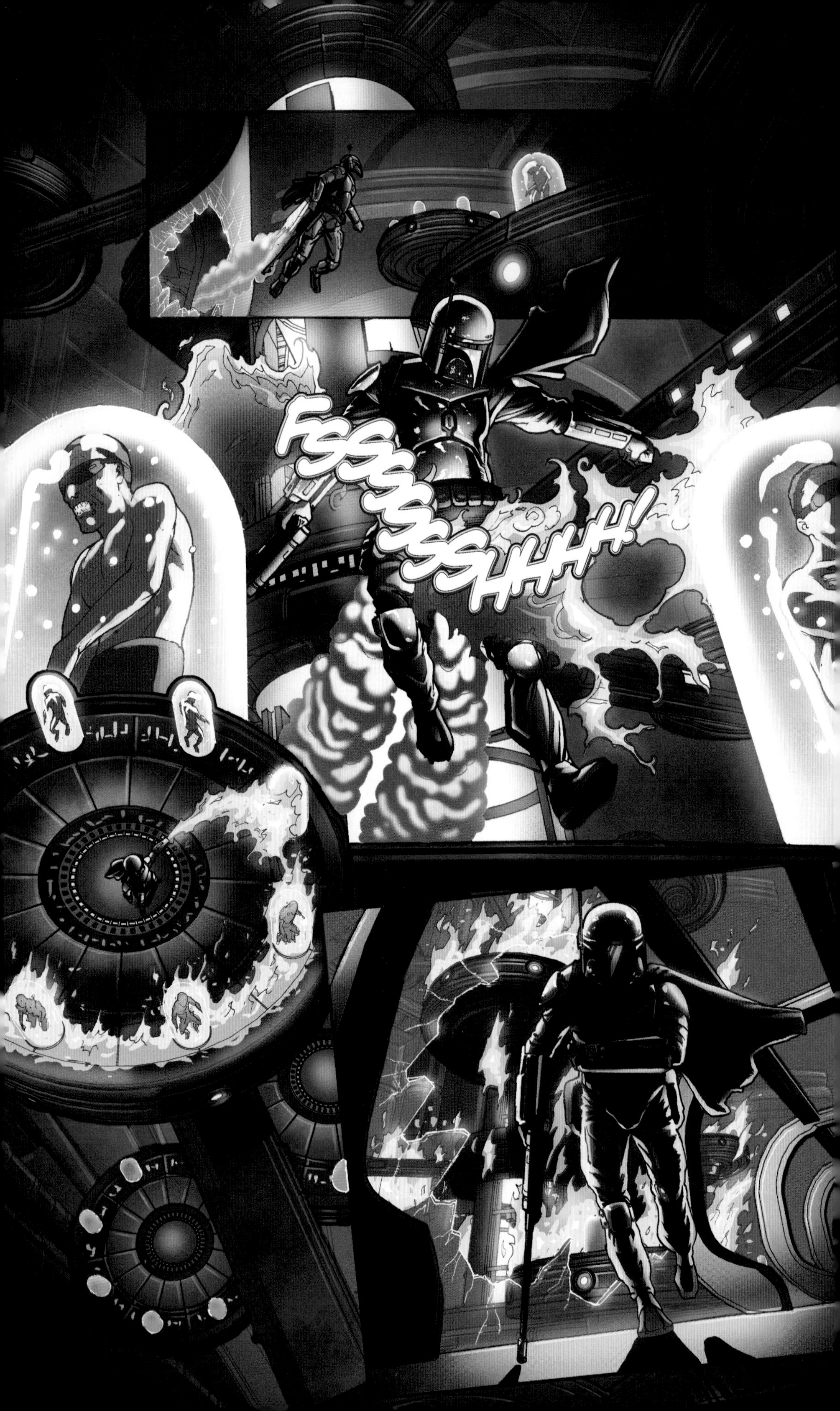
FSSSSSSSHHHHH!

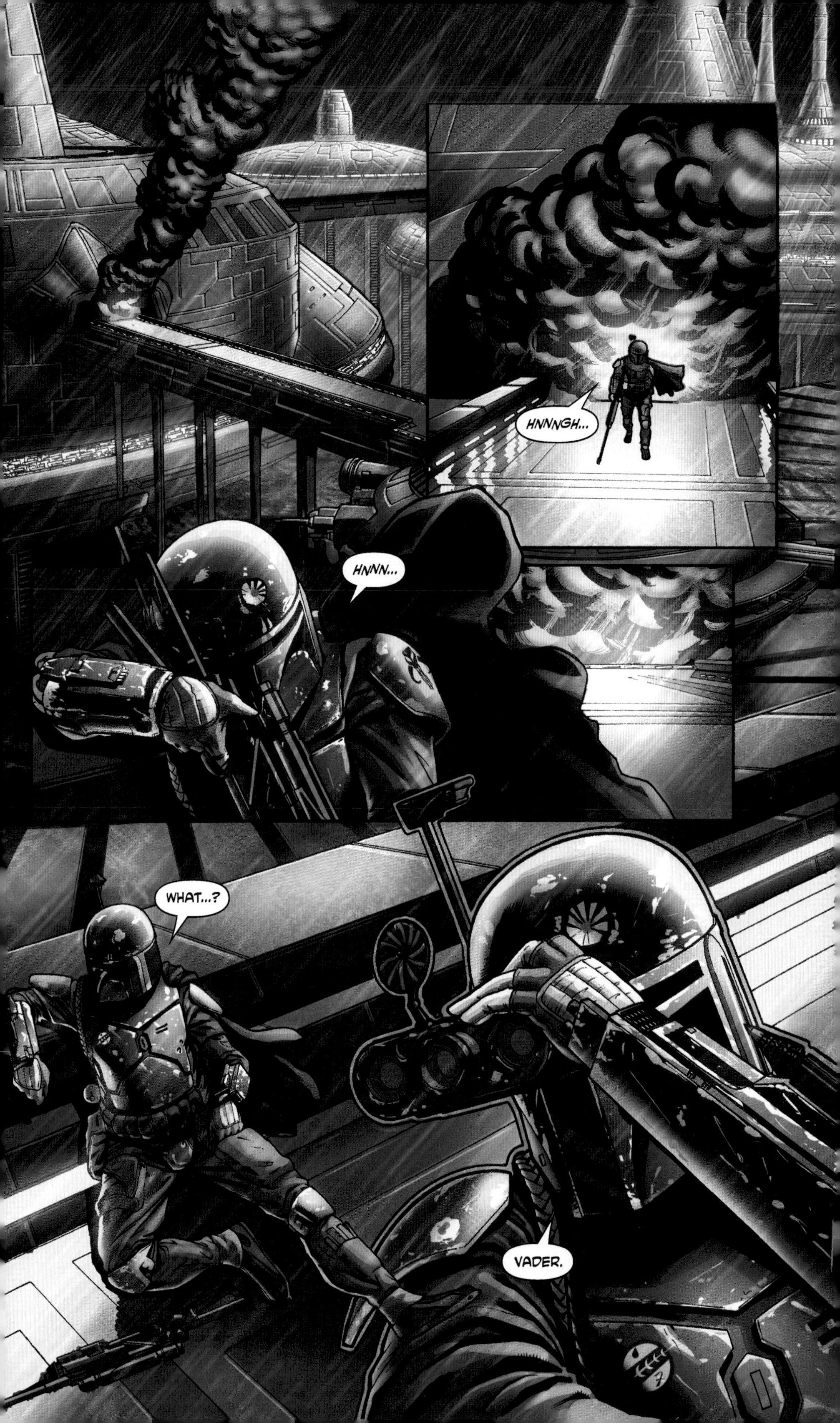
HNNNGH...
HNNN...
WHAT...?
VADER.

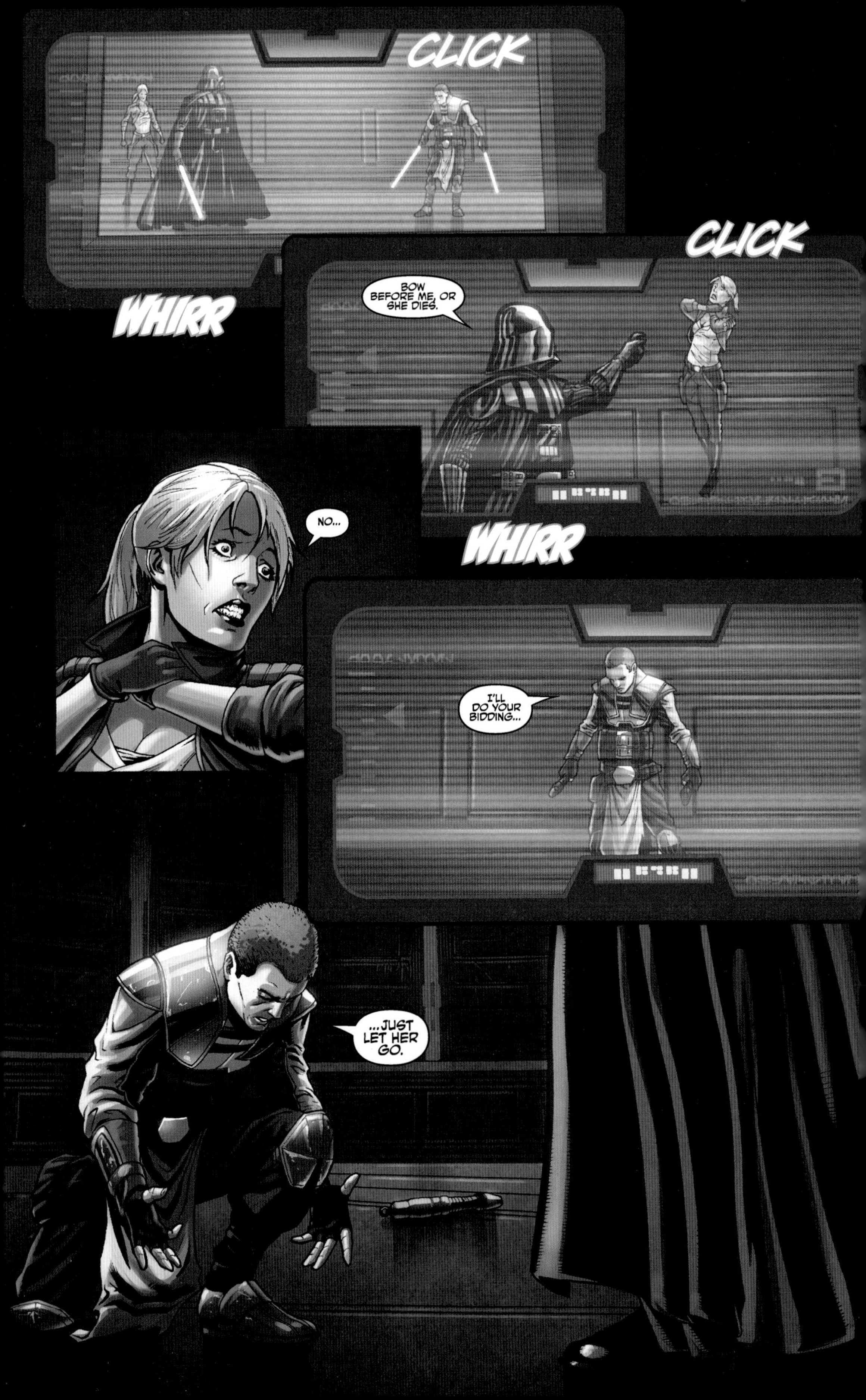
CLICK
WHIRR
CLICK
BOW BEFORE ME, OR SHE DIES.
NO...
WHIRR
I'LL DO YOUR BIDDING...
...JUST LET HER GO.

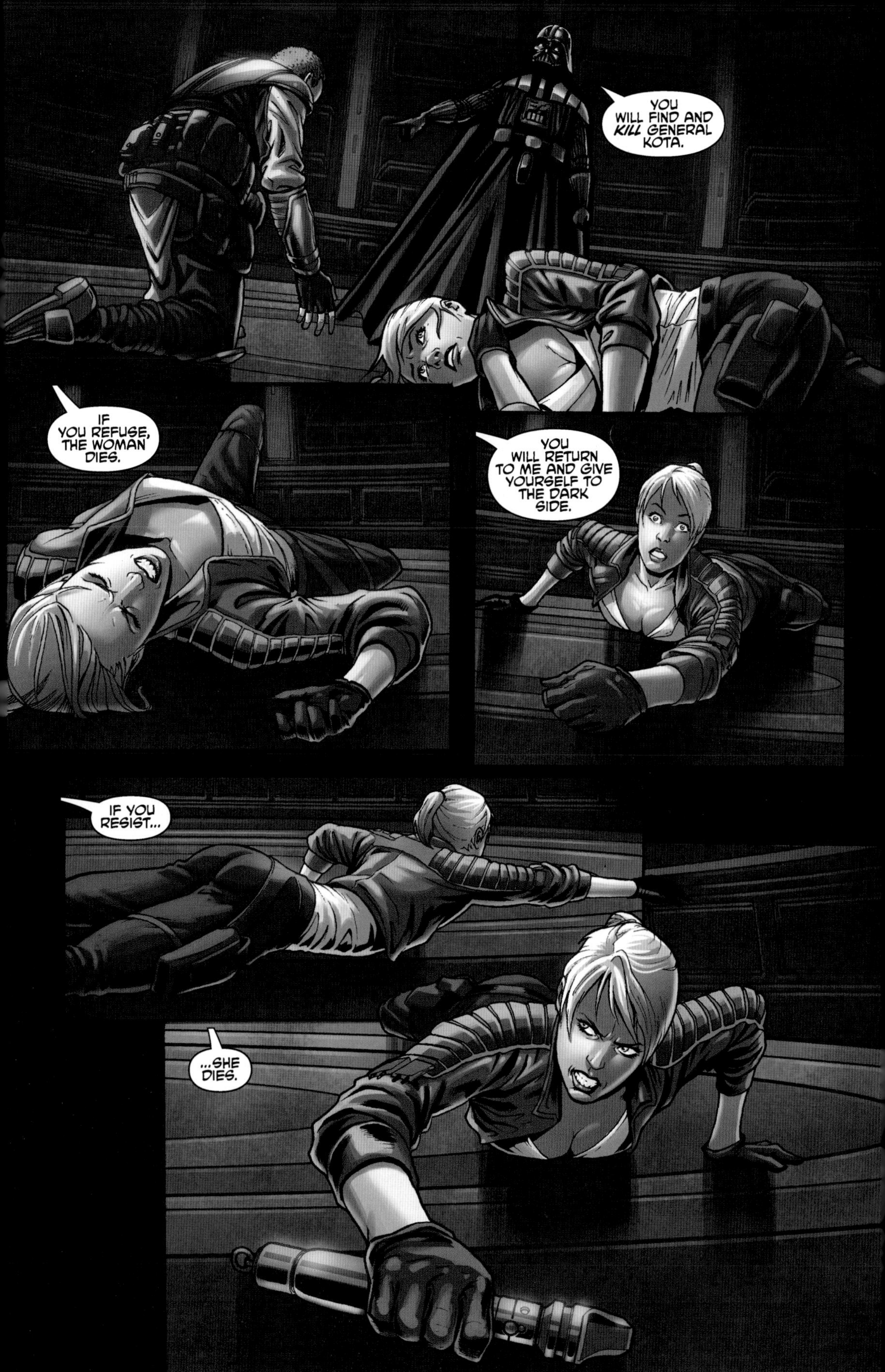
YOU WILL FIND AND *KILL* GENERAL KOTA.
IF YOU REFUSE, THE WOMAN DIES.
YOU WILL RETURN TO ME AND GIVE YOURSELF TO THE DARK SIDE.
IF YOU RESIST...
...SHE DIES.

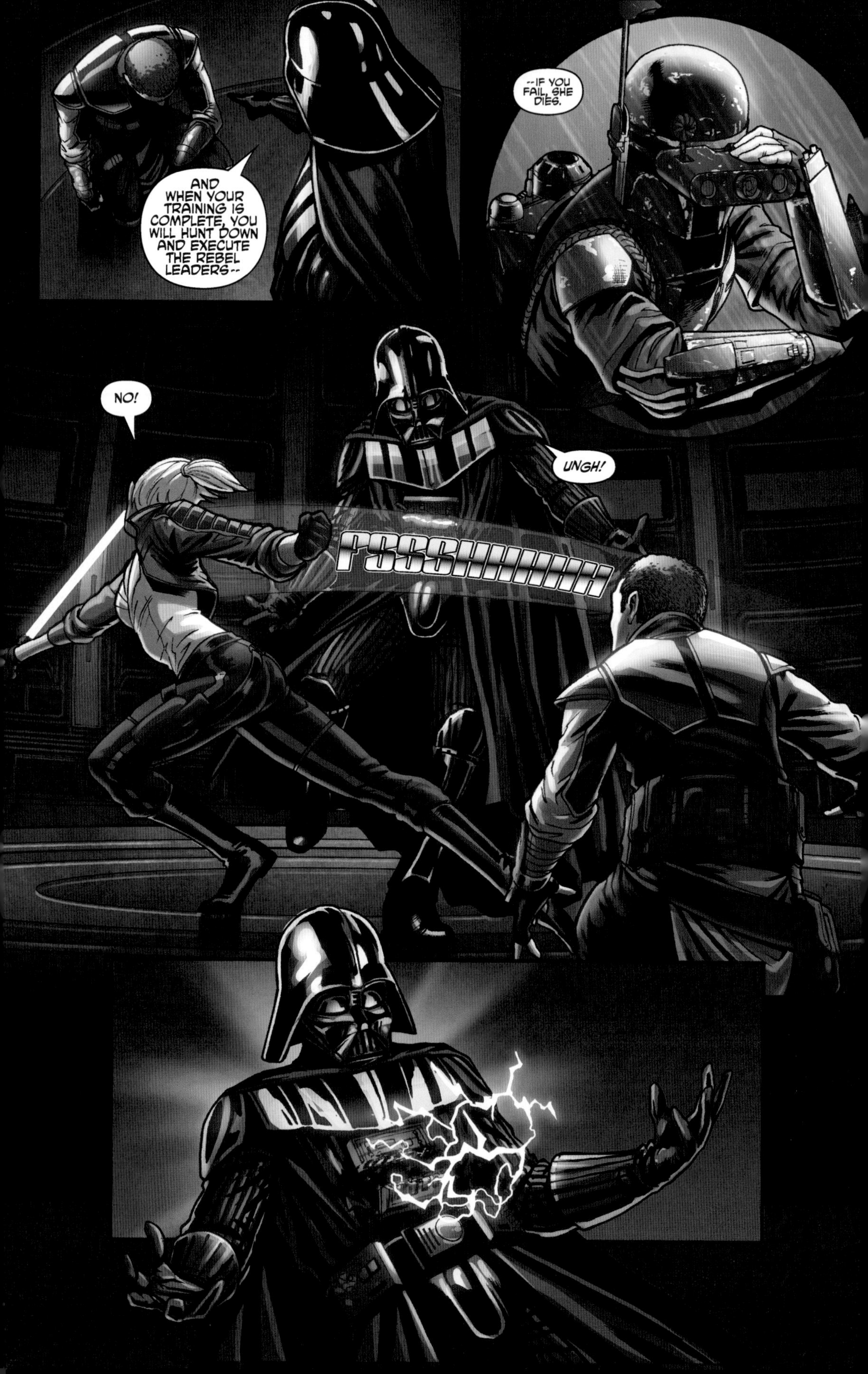
AND WHEN YOUR TRAINING IS COMPLETE, YOU WILL HUNT DOWN AND EXECUTE THE REBEL LEADERS--
--IF YOU FAIL, SHE DIES.
NO!
UNGH!
FSSSHHHHH

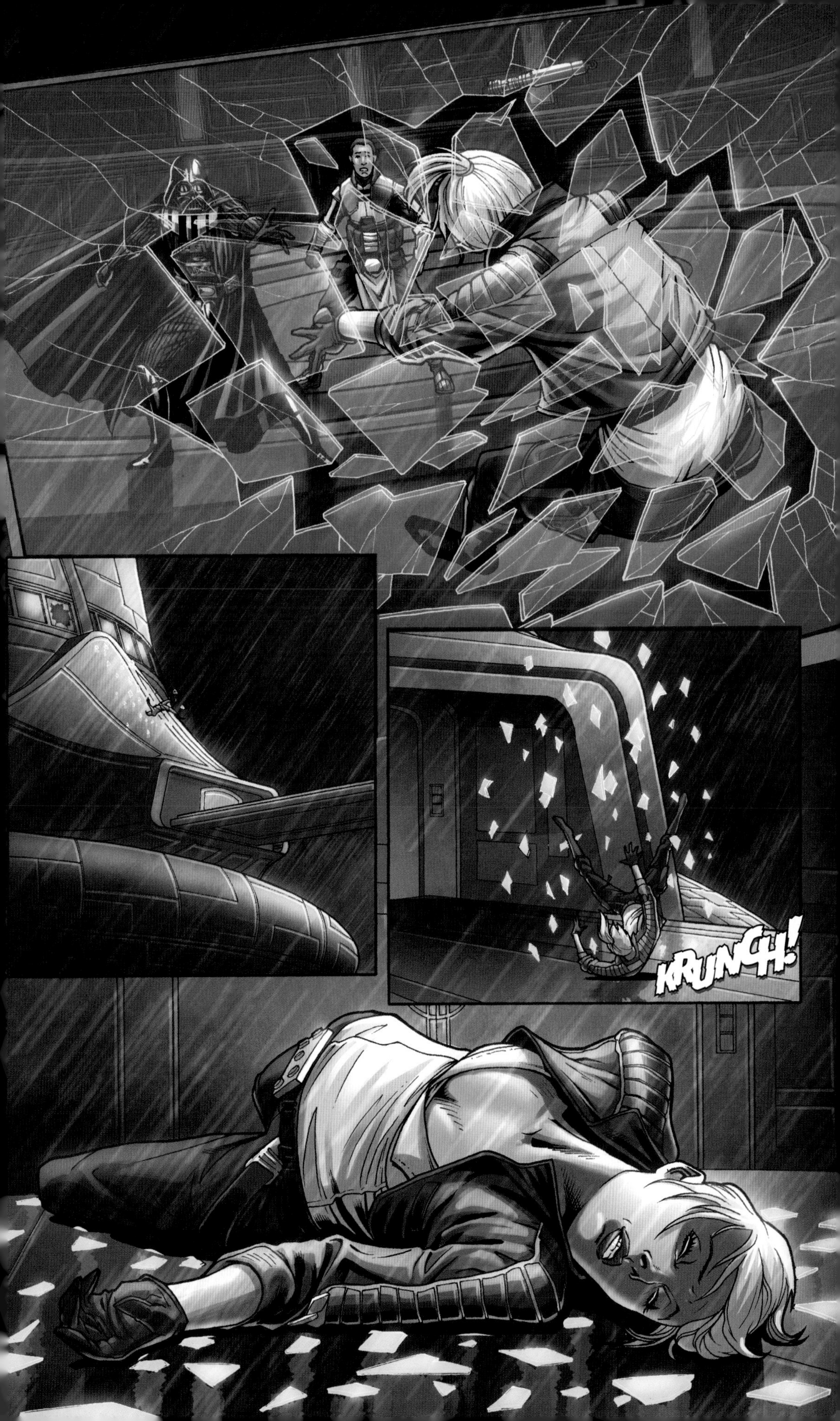
KRUNCH!

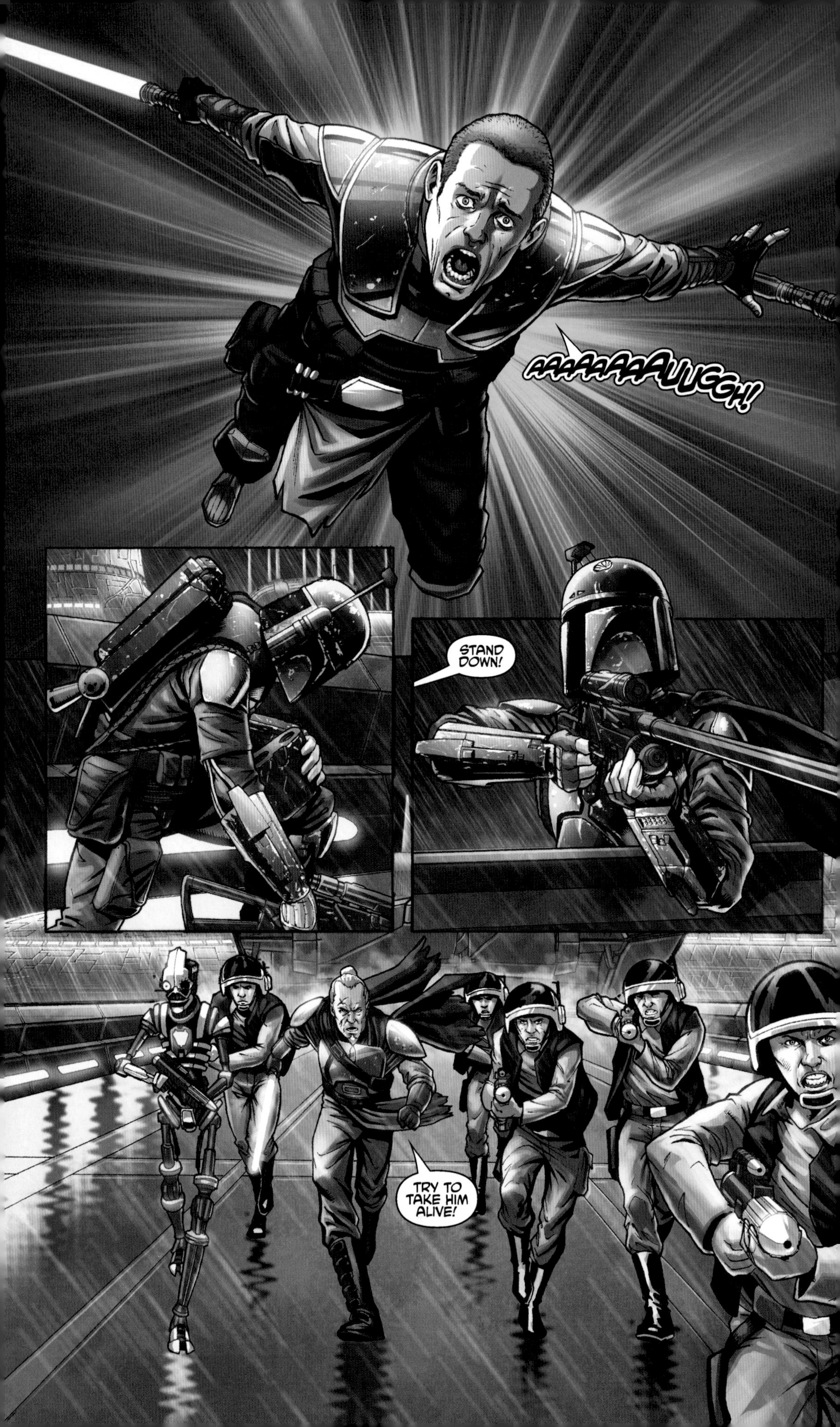
AAAAAAAAUUGGH!
STAND DOWN!
TRY TO TAKE HIM ALIVE!

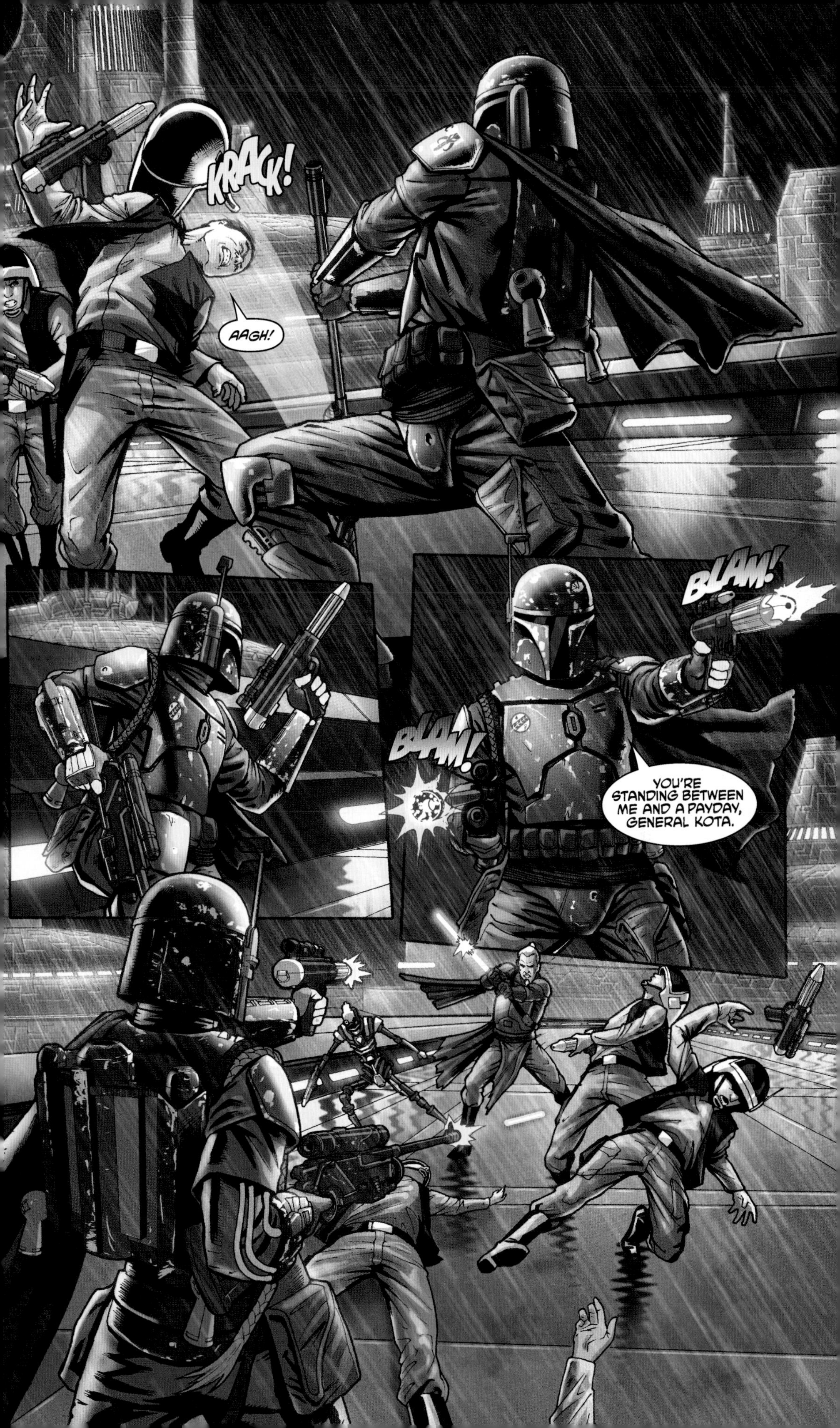
KRACK!
AAGH!
BLAM!
BLAM!
YOU'RE STANDING BETWEEN ME AND A PAYDAY, GENERAL KOTA.

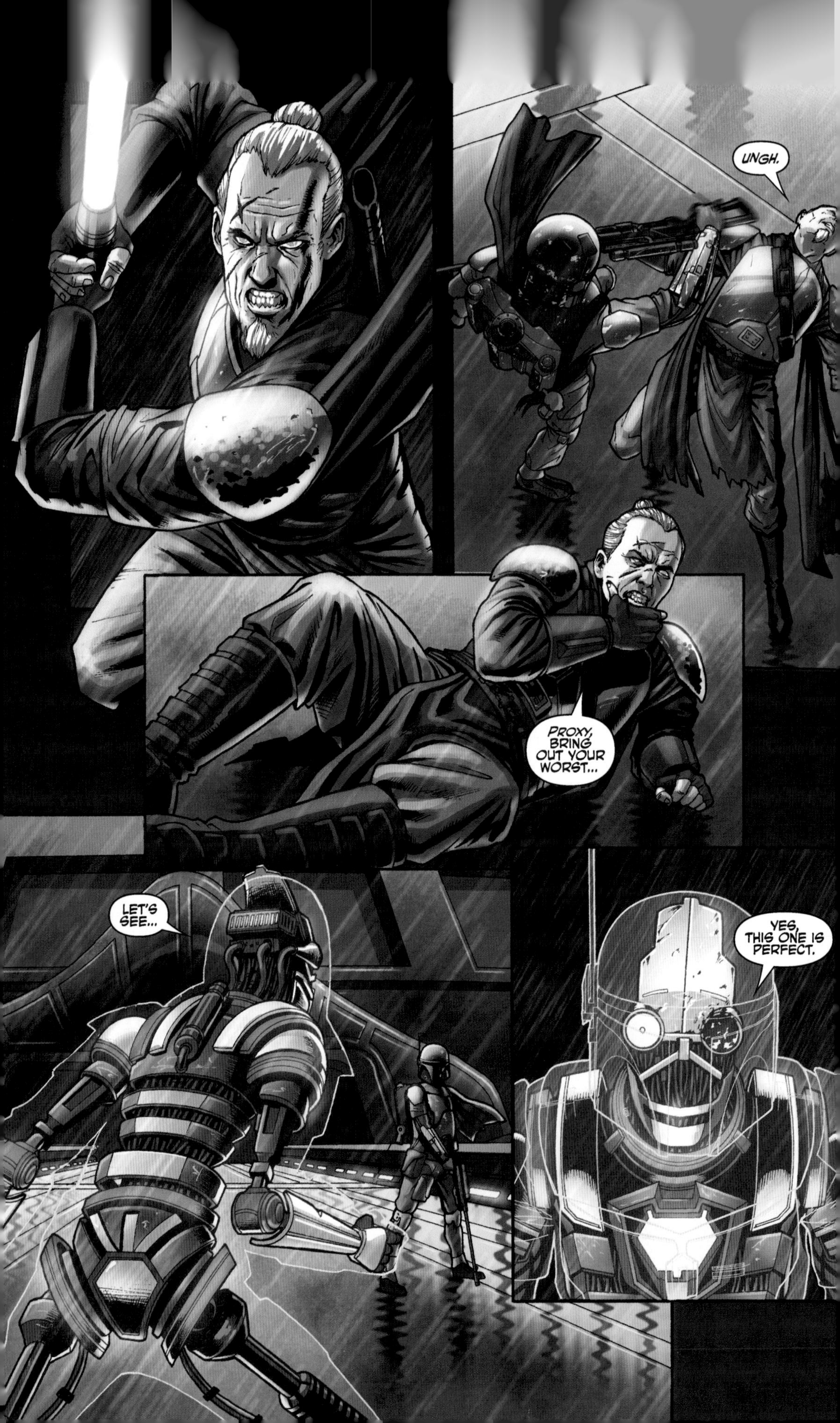
UNGH.
PROXY, BRING OUT YOUR WORST...
LET'S SEE...
YES, THIS ONE IS PERFECT.

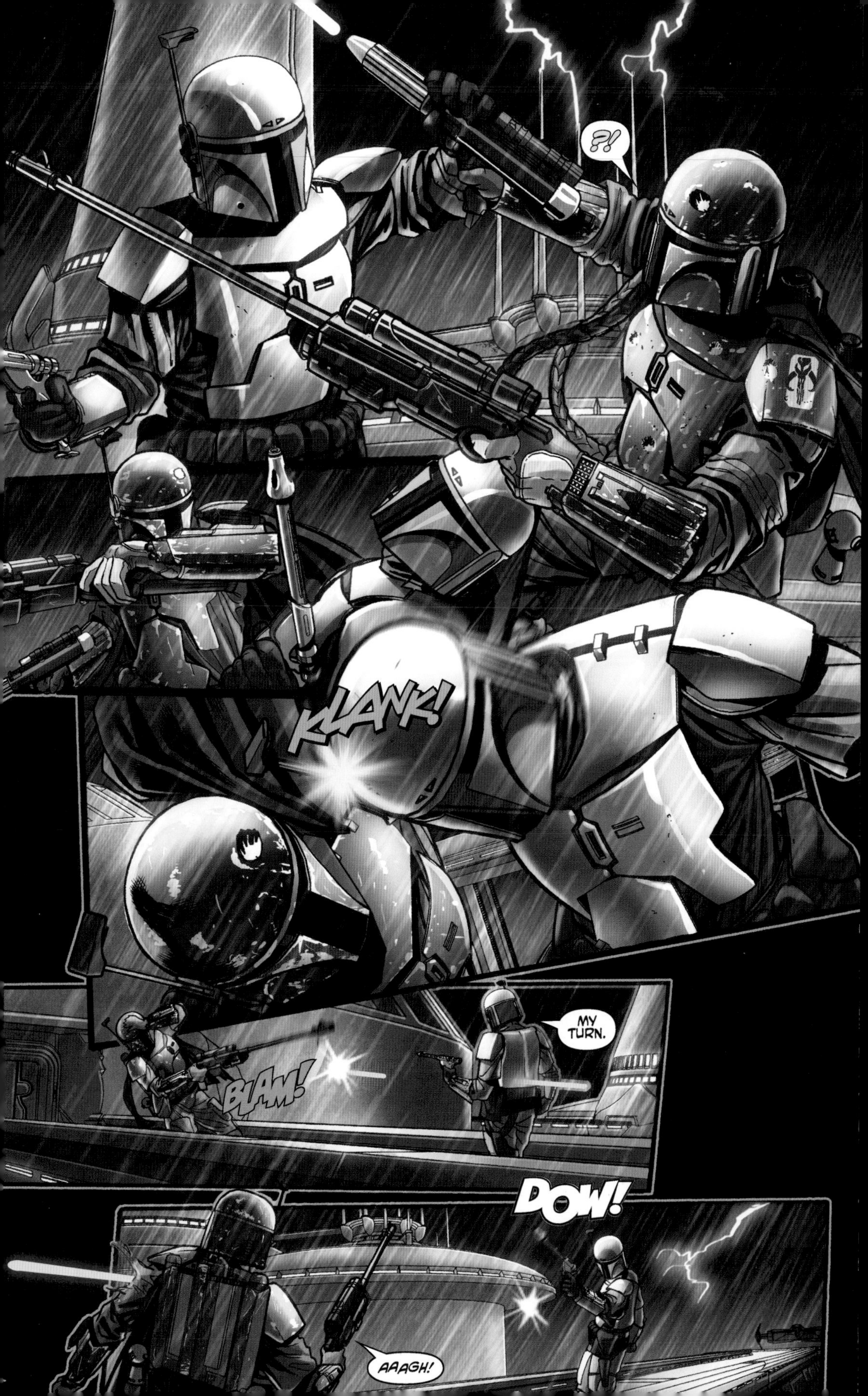
?!
KLANK!
MY TURN.
BLAM!
DOW!
AAAGH!

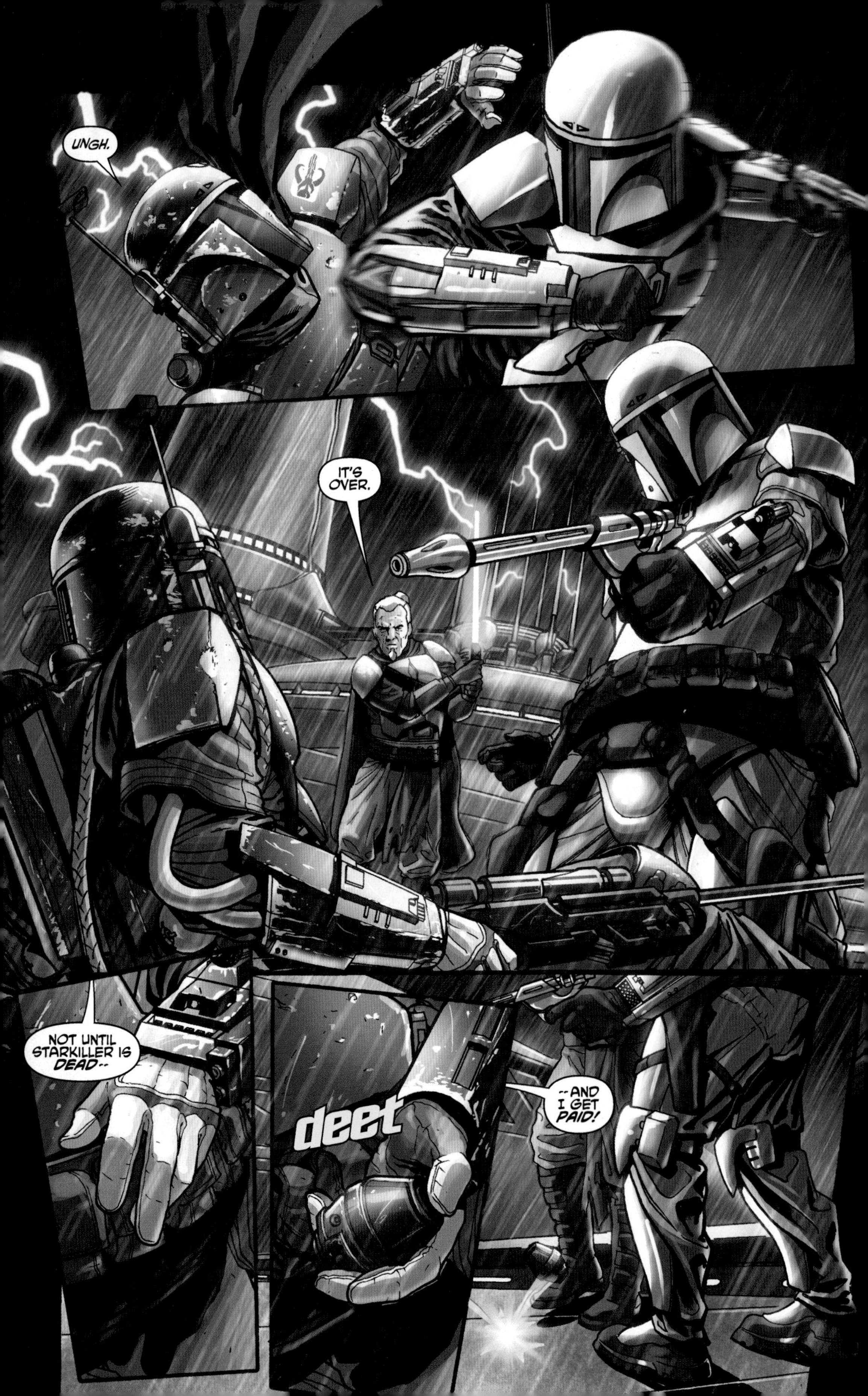
UNGH.
IT'S OVER.
NOT UNTIL STARKILLER IS *DEAD*--
deet
--AND I GET *PAID!*

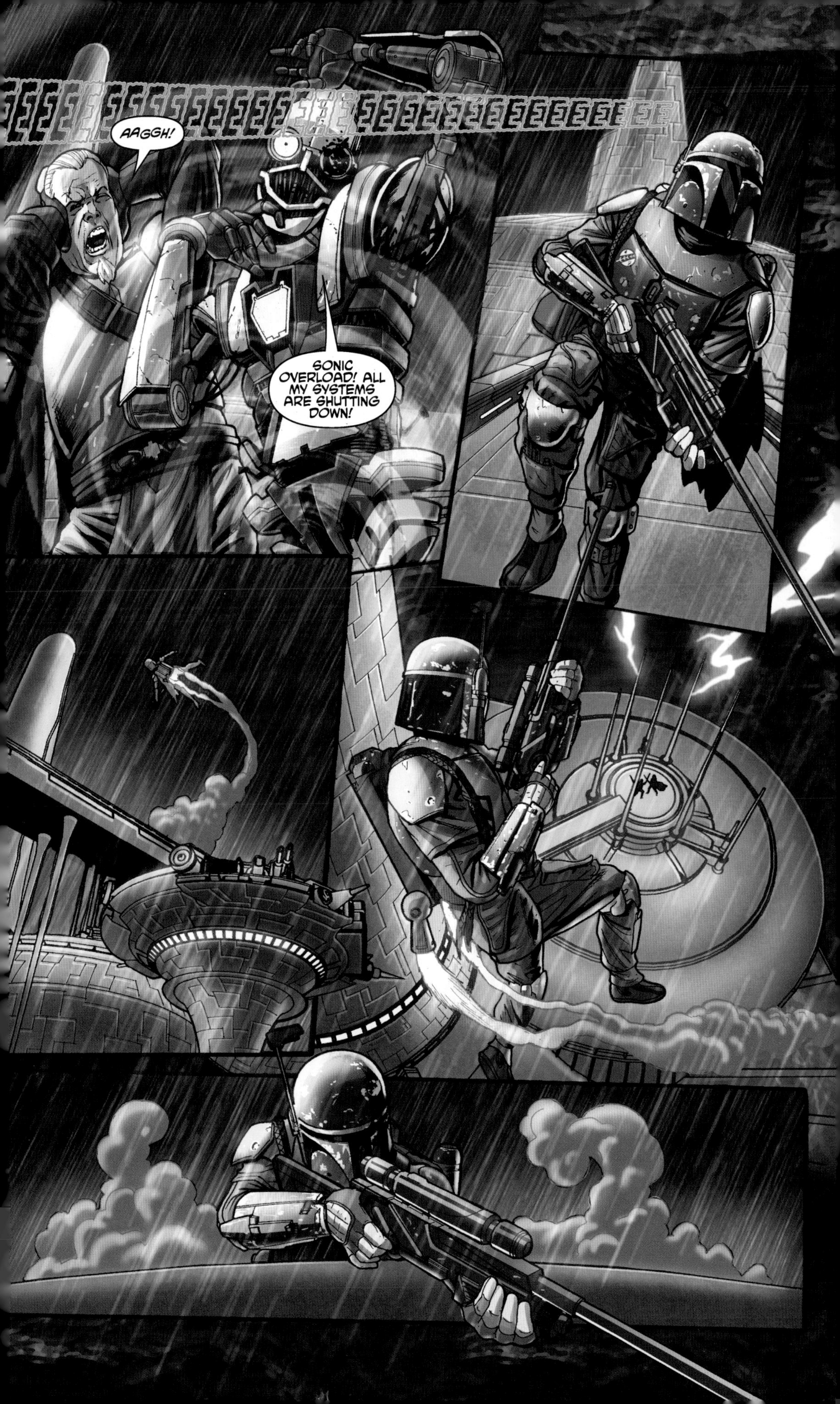
EEEEEEEEEEEEEEEEEEEEEEEEEEEEEEEEEEEE
AAGGH!
SONIC OVERLOAD! ALL MY SYSTEMS ARE SHUTTING DOWN!

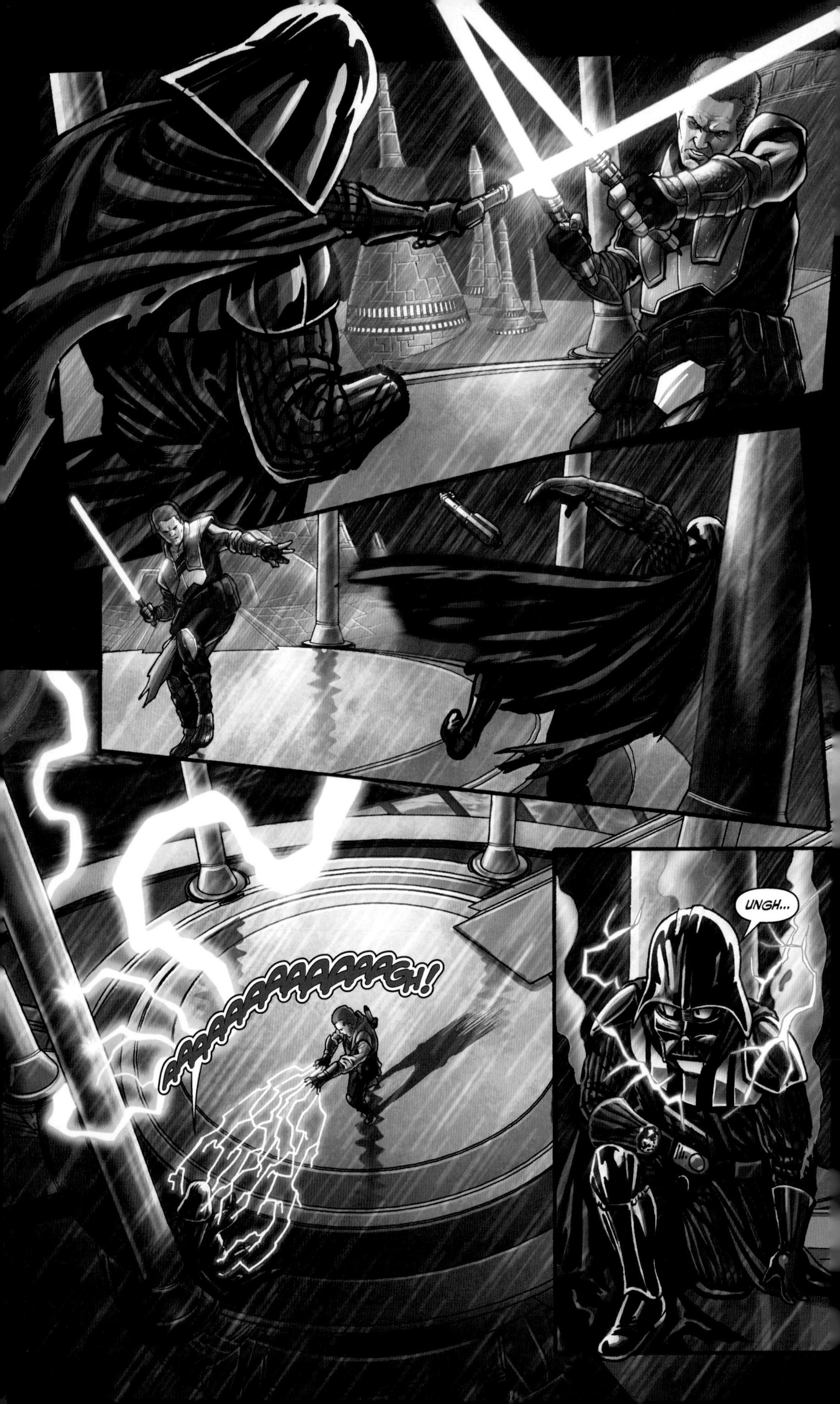
AAAAAAAAAAAAAAAAAGH!
UNGH...

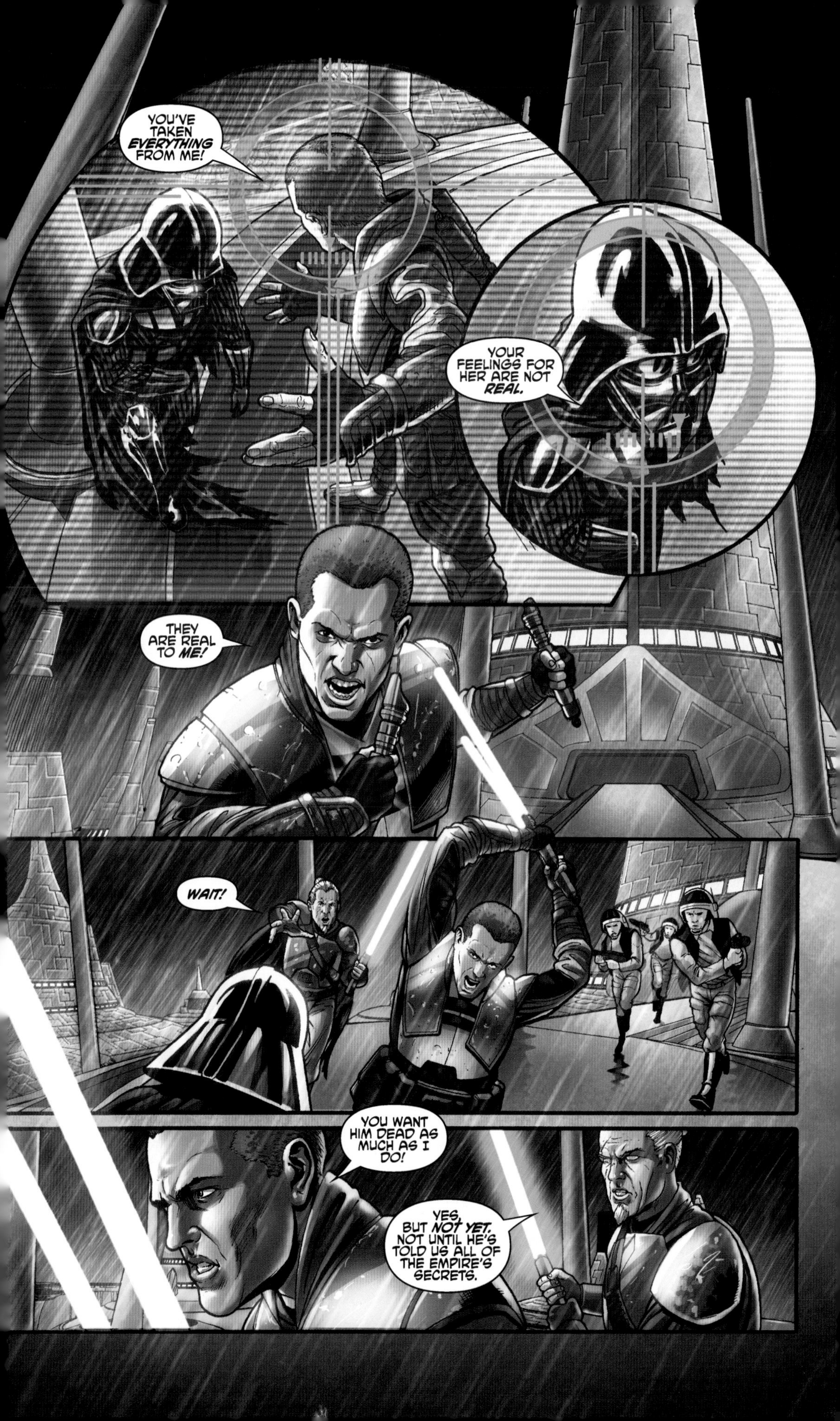
YOU'VE TAKEN *EVERYTHING* FROM ME!
YOUR FEELINGS FOR HER ARE NOT *REAL.*
THEY ARE REAL TO *ME!*
WAIT!
YOU WANT HIM DEAD AS MUCH AS I DO!
YES, BUT *NOT YET.* NOT UNTIL HE'S TOLD US ALL OF THE EMPIRE'S SECRETS.

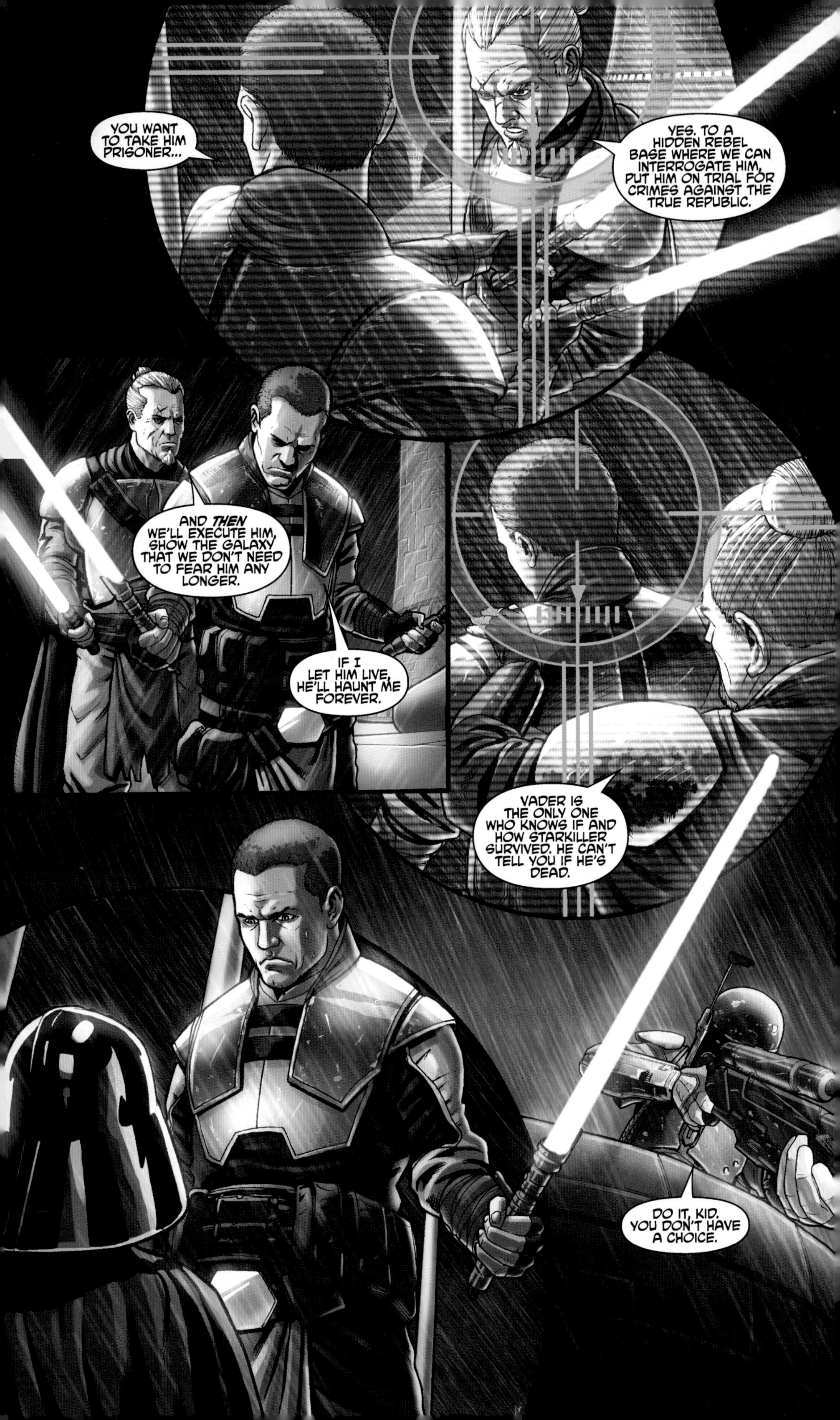
YOU WANT TO TAKE HIM PRISONER...
YES. TO A HIDDEN REBEL BASE WHERE WE CAN INTERROGATE HIM, PUT HIM ON TRIAL FOR CRIMES AGAINST THE TRUE REPUBLIC.
AND *THEN* WE'LL EXECUTE HIM, SHOW THE GALAXY THAT WE DON'T NEED TO FEAR HIM ANY LONGER.
IF I LET HIM LIVE, HE'LL HAUNT ME FOREVER.
VADER IS THE ONLY ONE WHO KNOWS IF AND HOW STARKILLER SURVIVED. HE CAN'T TELL YOU IF HE'S DEAD.
DO IT, KID. YOU DON'T HAVE A CHOICE.

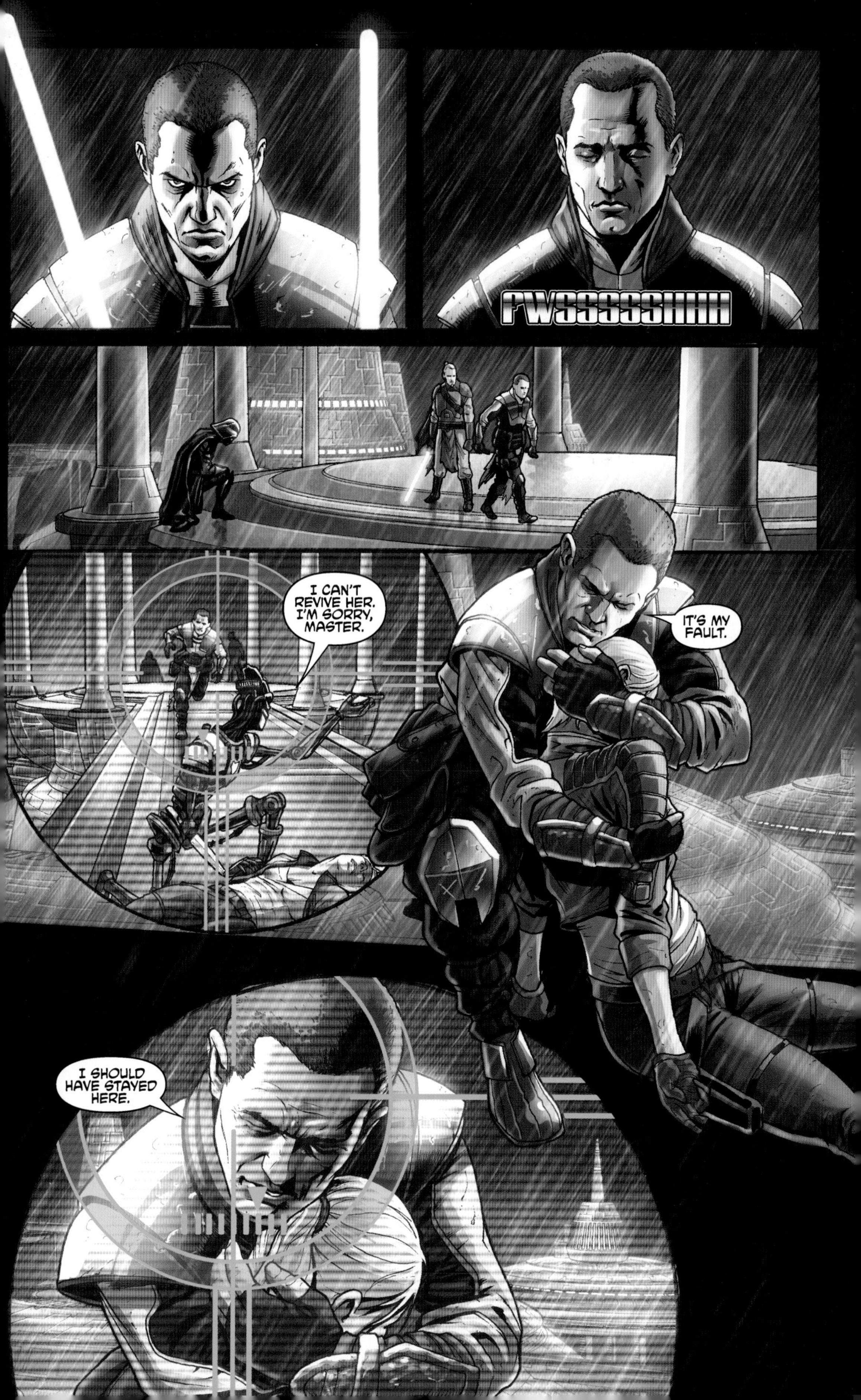
FWSSSSSHHHH
I CAN'T REVIVE HER. I'M SORRY, MASTER.
IT'S MY FAULT.
I SHOULD HAVE STAYED HERE.

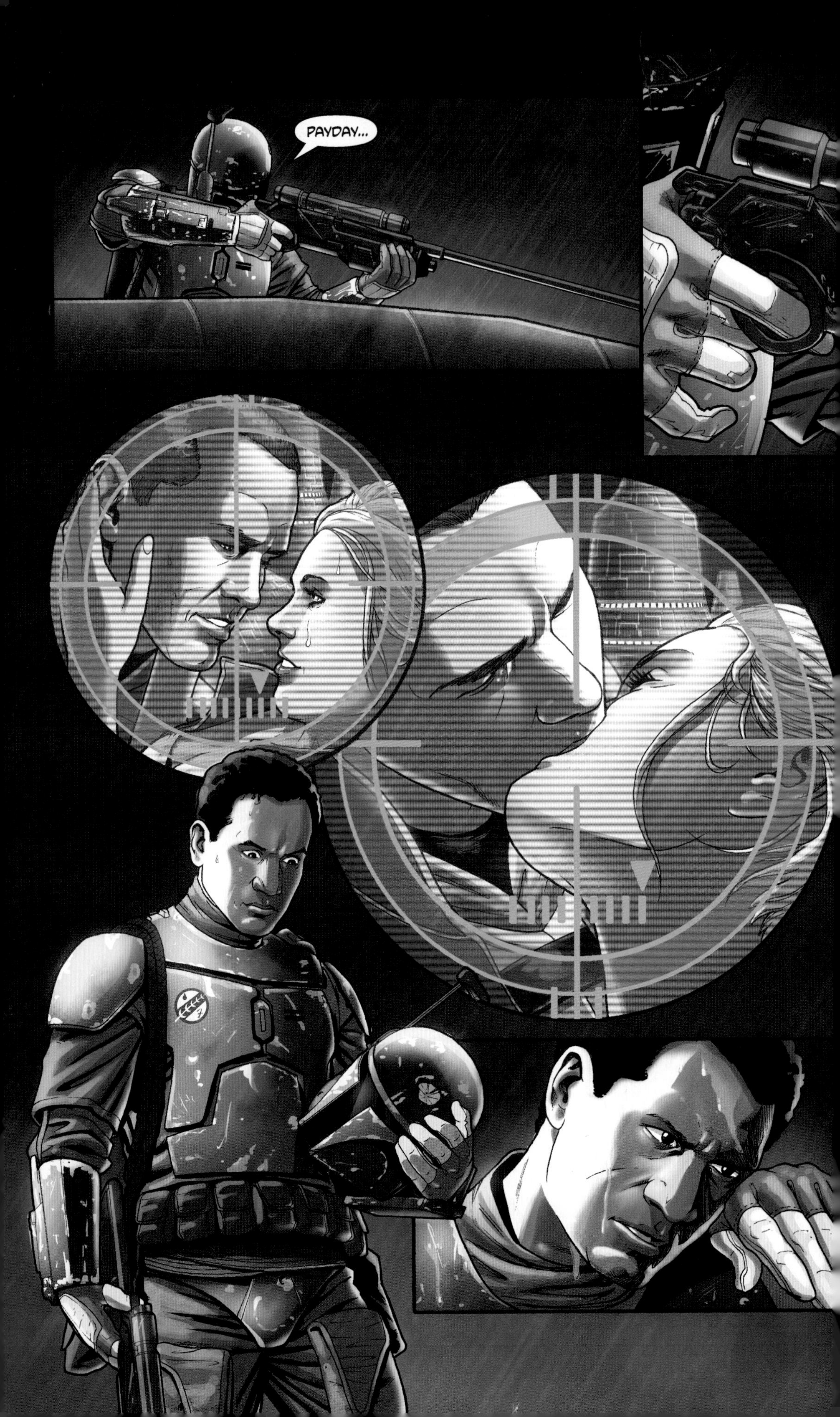
PAYDAY...

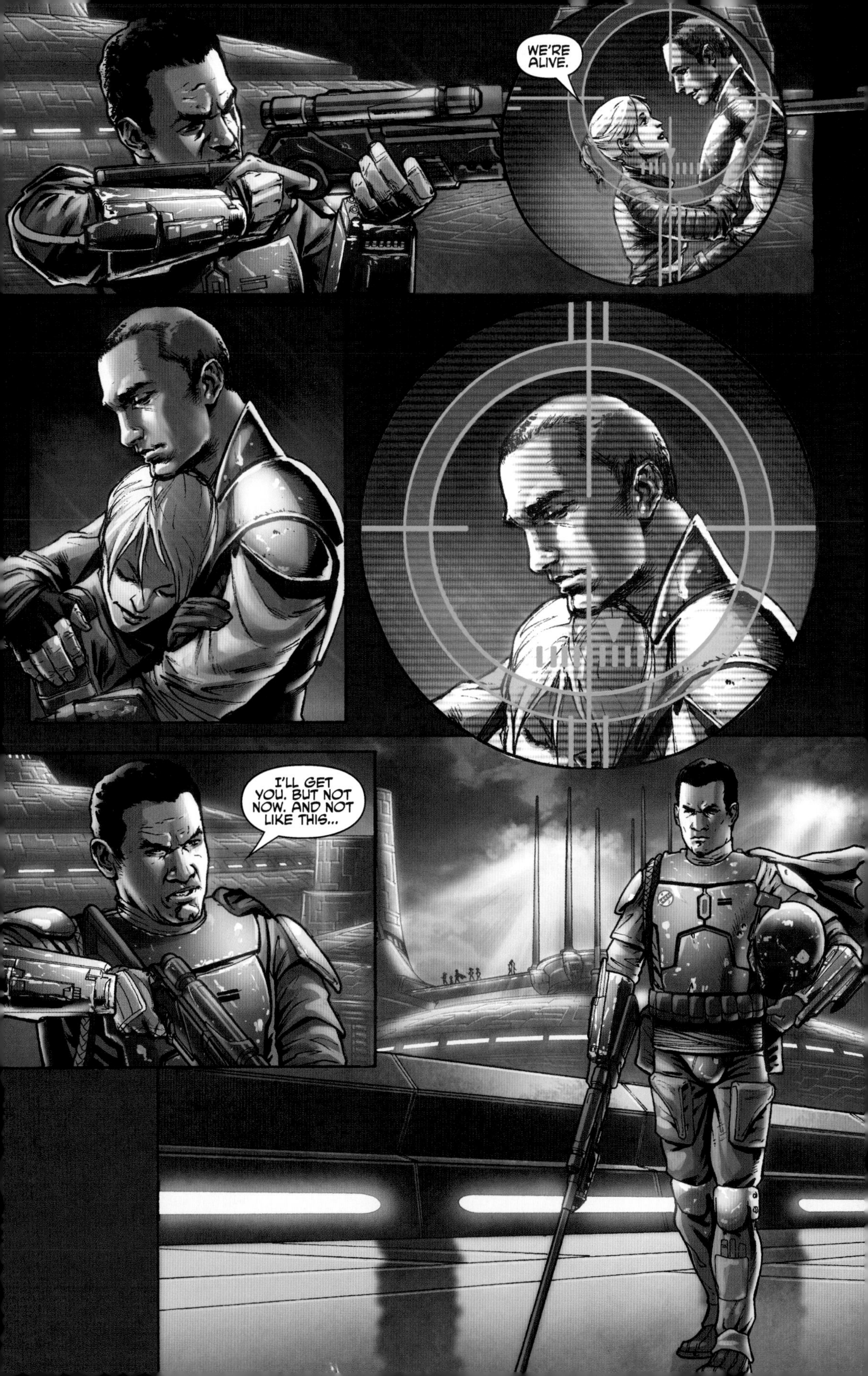
WE'RE ALIVE.
I'LL GET YOU. BUT NOT NOW. AND NOT LIKE THIS...

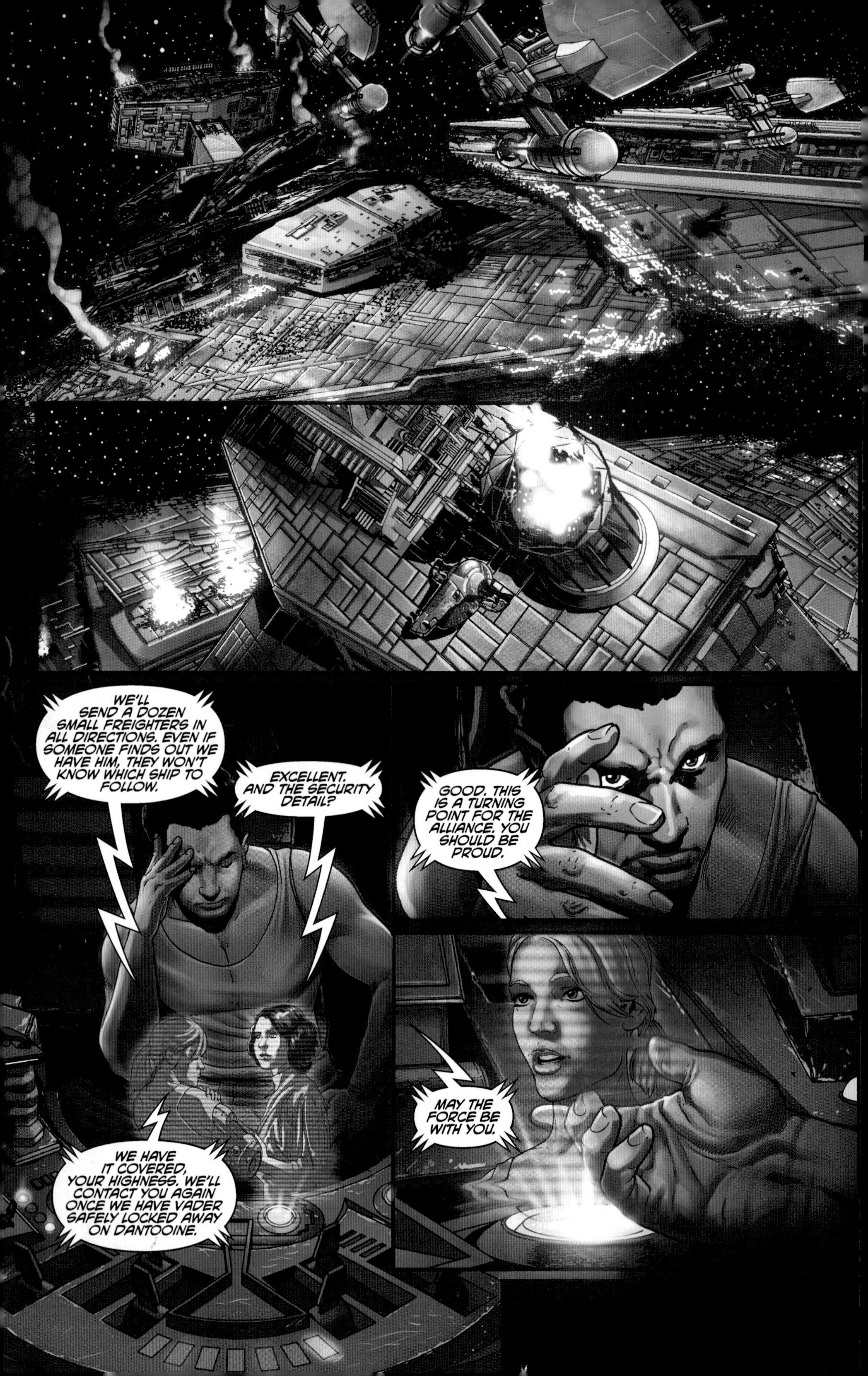
WE'LL SEND A DOZEN SMALL FREIGHTERS IN ALL DIRECTIONS. EVEN IF SOMEONE FINDS OUT WE HAVE HIM, THEY WON'T KNOW WHICH SHIP TO FOLLOW.
EXCELLENT. AND THE SECURITY DETAIL?
WE HAVE IT COVERED, YOUR HIGHNESS. WE'LL CONTACT YOU AGAIN ONCE WE HAVE VADER SAFELY LOCKED AWAY ON DANTOOINE.
GOOD. THIS IS A TURNING POINT FOR THE ALLIANCE. YOU SHOULD BE PROUD.
MAY THE FORCE BE WITH YOU.

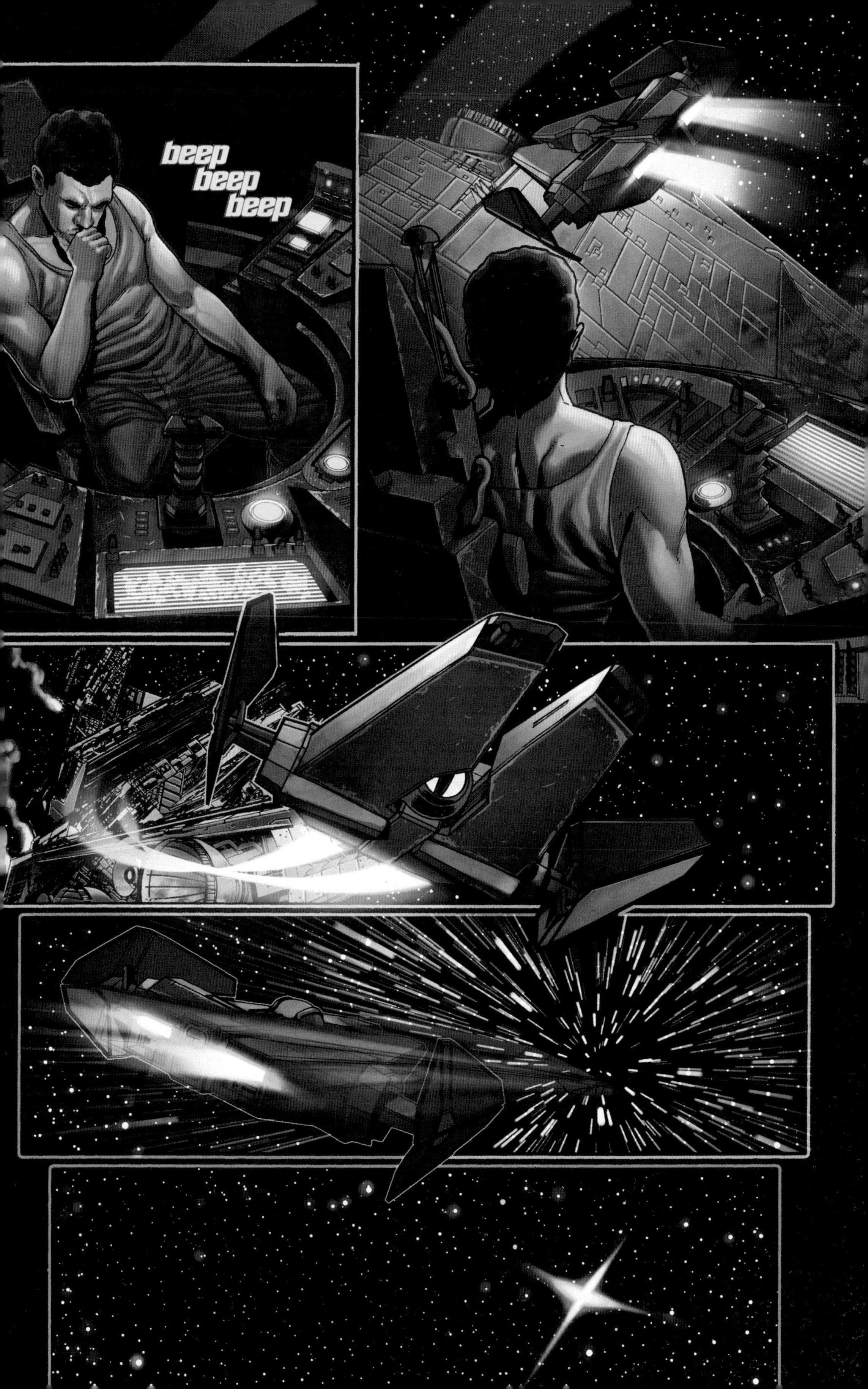
beep beep beep

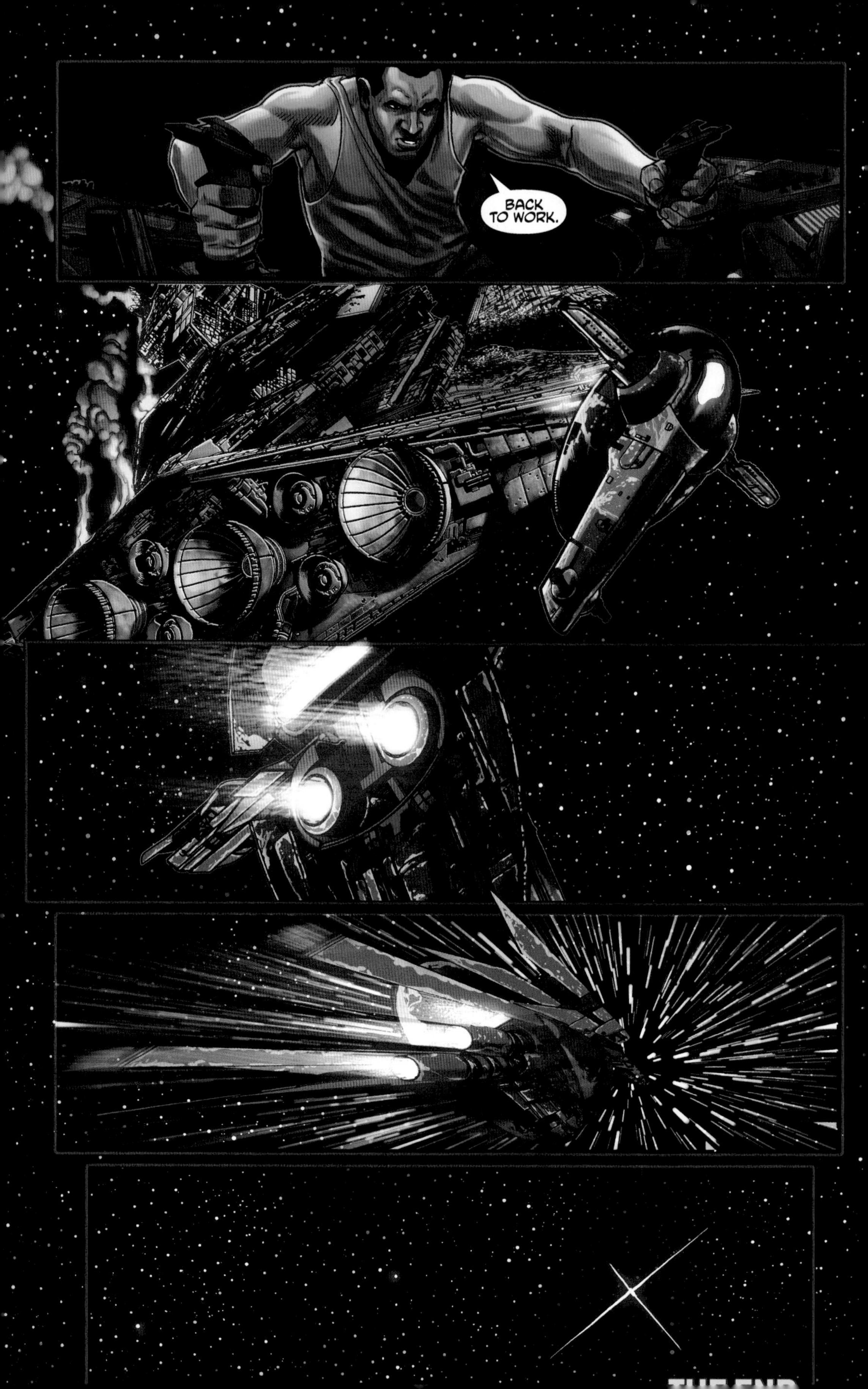
BACK TO WORK.

STAR WARS GRAPHIC NOVEL TIMELINE (IN YEARS)

Omnibus: Tales of the Jedi—5,000–3,986 BSW4

Knights of the Old Republic (9 volumes)—3,964 BSW4

Jedi vs. Sith—1,000 BSW4

Omnibus: Rise of the Sith—33 BSW4

Episode I: The Phantom Menace—32 BSW4

Omnibus: Emissaries and Assassins—32 BSW4

Bounty Hunters—31 BSW4

Omnibus: Quinlan Vos – Jedi in Darkness—31–28 BSW4

Omnibus: Menace Revealed—31–22 BSW4

Honor and Duty—24 BSW4

Episode II: Attack of the Clones—22 BSW4

Clone Wars (9 volumes)—22–19 BSW4

Clone Wars Adventures (10 volumes)—22–19 BSW4

The Clone Wars (7 volumes)—22–19 BSW4

General Grievous—20 BSW4

Episode III: Revenge of the Sith—19 BSW4

Dark Times (4 volumes)—19 BSW4

Omnibus: Droids—3 BSW4

Omnibus: Boba Fett—3–1 BSW4, 0–10 ASW4

The Force Unleashed—2 BSW4

Adventures (4 volumes)—1–0 BSW4, 0–3 ASW4

Episode IV: A New Hope—SW4

Classic Star Wars—0–3 ASW4

A Long Time Ago… (7 volumes)—0–4 ASW4

Empire (6 volumes)—0 ASW4

Rebellion (3 volumes)—0 ASW4

Omnibus: Early Victories—0–1 ASW4

Jabba the Hutt: The Art of the Deal—1 ASW4

Episode V: The Empire Strikes Back—3 ASW4

Omnibus: Shadows of the Empire—3.5–4.5 ASW4

Episode VI: Return of the Jedi—4 ASW4

Omnibus: X-Wing Rogue Squadron—4–5 ASW4

The Thrawn Trilogy—9 ASW4

Dark Empire—10 ASW4

Crimson Empire—11 ASW4

Jedi Academy: Leviathan—13 ASW4

Union—20 ASW4

Chewbacca—25 ASW4

Legacy (10 volumes)—130 ASW4

Old Republic Era
25,000 – 1000 years before
Star Wars: A New Hope

Rise of the Empire Era
1000 – 0 years before
Star Wars: A New Hope

Rebellion Era
0 – 5 years after
Star Wars: A New Hope

New Republic Era
5 – 25 years after
Star Wars: A New Hope

New Jedi Order Era
25+ years after
Star Wars: A New Hope

Legacy Era
130+ years after
Star Wars: A New Hope

Infinities
Does not apply to timeline

Sergio Aragonés Stomps Star Wars
Star Wars Tales
Star Wars Infinities
Tag and Bink
Star Wars Visionaries

SW4 = before *Episode IV: A New Hope*. ASW4 = after *Episode IV: A New Hope*.

STAR WARS®
EMPIRE

DARK HORSE COMICS

TO FIND A COMICS SHOP IN YOUR AREA, CALL 1-888-266-4226.

For more information or to order direct:
*On the web: darkhorse.com
*E-mail: mailorder@darkhorse.com
*Phone: 1-800-862-0052 Mon.-Fri. 9 A.M. to 5 P.M. Pacific Time.

*prices and availability subject to change without notice. STAR WARS © 2010 Lucasfilm Ltd. & TM (BL 8017)